The Book of Deuteronomy and Post-modern Christianity

The Book of Deuteronomy
and Post-modern Christianity

by James W. Baxter

RESOURCE *Publications* • Eugene, Oregon

THE BOOK OF DEUTERONOMY AND POST-MODERN CHRISTIANITY

Copyright © 2013 James W. Baxter. All rights reserved. Except for brief quotations in critical publications or reviews, no part of this book may be reproduced in any manner without prior written permission from the publisher. Write: Permissions, Wipf and Stock Publishers, 199 W. 8th Ave., Suite 3, Eugene, OR 97401.

Resource Publications
An Imprint of Wipf and Stock Publishers
199 W. 8th Ave., Suite 3
Eugene, OR 97401
www.wipfandstock.com

ISBN 13: 978-1-62032-306-9

Manufactured in the U.S.A.

All scripture excerpts are from the New Revised Standard Version Bible, copyright 1989, division of Christian Education of the National Council of the Churches of Christ in the U.S.

To Dr. Walter Brueggemann, with admiration

Table of Contents

Author's Note   ix
Preface   xi
Acknowledgments   xiii

Chapter 1	Why the Hebrew Scriptures?	1
Chapter 2	Why Post-modern Christianity?	4
Chapter 3	Background to Deuteronomy	10
Chapter 4	The Setting and the Basics	16
Chapter 5	Whys and Wherefores	26
Chapter 6	More Preamble	33
Chapter 7	Right Living: The Statutes and Ordinances	48
Chapter 8	Do's and Don'ts	55
Chapter 9	Take Time to Be Holy	65
Chapter 10	Justice: True, Honest Justice	70
Chapter 11	How to Do a War	88
Chapter 12	How to be Neighborly	94
Chapter 13	Who's In and Who's Out	102
Chapter 14	The Summation	105

Annotated Bibliography   111

Author's Note

I HAVE WRITTEN THIS book for the layperson with an interest in Christianity and/or the Hebrew scriptures. Since it is not an academic work, I have not cited the statements and opinions contained herein. For the most part, except for material related to post-modern Christianity, I have drawn the commentary directly from Dr. Brueggemann's *Deuteronomy*. The version of post-modern Christianity presented here is my own compilation, taken from other sources listed in the bibliography.

Why post-modern Christianity? Traditional Christianity can no longer address the massive changes our society is undergoing. A new understanding of God that is compatible with our emerging understanding of our society and of the universe is required.

Why Deuteronomy? This will become clear in the body of the book. Deuteronomy ultimately formed the basis of Western society: its teachings provide the groundwork for our laws and justice system, our social structure, and the ideals that drive our interactions. This ancient wisdom is every bit as relevant to our lives today, even with the societal upheavals we are experiencing, as it was when it was written.

Preface

THE HISTORICAL JESUS OF Nazareth was an itinerate preacher, one of many in his day in the region of Galilee. Unlike most of his peers, however, his preaching mainly focused on the injustices fostered by the rich upon the poor of his society. He provoked the rich and powerful, challenging their self-declared importance and control over others. Naturally, both the Jewish and Roman leadership found this type of preaching unsettling, especially after Jesus became a high-profile figure.

As his influence grew, the establishment felt it necessary to eliminate him to preserve their status quo. We don't know a great deal about Jesus' life, but we do know that his followers abandoned him when he was seized. We also know that after that, they came back together and, *at risk to their own lives*, continued Jesus' mission. As followers of The Way, as Jesus' group was known initially, these early Christians risked death to pursue their spiritual path. It is difficult today to imagine such passion, commitment, and strength. The early church must have been immersed in some incredibly strong force, something that entirely consumed the lives of its members. What was it? What happened to it? Where did it go? Would Christians today risk death for their church?

Maybe we no longer have to die for what we know in our hearts, but the same life-changing power that Jesus seemed to have is still around, as strong as ever and just as accessible. There is a problem, however. Though Deuteronomy beautifully describes the power of the heart that Jesus had, this lies in the context of the cosmos as known two- to three-thousand years ago. Post-modern thinking describes our cosmos and lives as we know them today. Perhaps by applying post-modern thinking to three-thousand-year-old wisdom, we can open new avenues for those of us seeking deeper meaning to life. This book is an exploration of such a marriage. Welcome to the journey.

Acknowledgments

I HAVE BASED THE biblical commentary of this book almost entirely on *Deuteronomy* by Walter Brueggemann, the William Marcellus McPheeters Professor Emeritus of Old Testament at Columbia Theological Seminary in Decatur, Georgia. I have extracted the text, with permission, from Dr. Brueggemann's work and rephrased it for the non-academic reader.

As an American Protestant Old Testament scholar and theologian, Walter Brueggemann is an important figure in progressive Christianity. He is widely considered one of the most influential Old Testament scholars of the last several decades, having written more than fifty-eight books, hundreds of articles, and several commentaries on books of the Bible. He is known throughout the world for his method of combining literary and sociological modes when reading the Bible.

I am indebted also to my editor Heather Conn, who asked many insightful questions, encouraged me, and was a delightful taskmaster. As well, I thank The Rev'd. Canon Dr. Harold Munn, Anglican Mentor in Residence, Vancouver School of Theology for his comments.

I further acknowledge my loving and patient wife Beverly, with whom I frequently engaged in lively discussions about theology, God, and everything.

Jim Baxter
Vancouver, B.C.
January 2013

Chapter 1

Why the Hebrew Scriptures?

JESUS WAS NOT A Christian. He did not even start Christianity. Rather, Jesus was Jewish, a rabbi intent on reforming the Judaism of his time. It is true, however, that Christianity grew out of the "Jesus movement" (those following him). As a result, Judaism and Christianity, from the start, were closely intertwined and remain so today. The two are sister-faith traditions; though they may appear to conflict in their respective understanding of God, they reflect deep agreement on most fundamental claims.

Therefore, we cannot seriously understand the Christian faith without also coming to know a great deal more about Judaism. And the bedrock of Judaism is found in the Hebrew scriptures.

The Shared History of Jews and Christians

The origins of Christianity lie in a sect of Judaism known as The Way, which grew out of the Jesus movement. The Way was just one of several such sects at that time. After the Romans destroyed Jerusalem in about 70 BCE (Before the Common/Christian Era), only a few of the several sects truly survived. One of these developed into the rabbinical Judaism that we know today; another, The Way, began to diverge into Christianity. But both traditions, having survived the same trauma, faced many of the same issues and pressures. Indeed, they have shared parallel development, the spiritual awareness of each growing in complementary ways.

In essence, Judaism and Christianity share the same story of God's revelation, which is expressed through psalms, prophets, the Pentateuch, and the wisdom literature. In these two traditions, human existence plays out in a down-to-earth story; that is, awareness of God is found through

Deuteronomy and Post-Modern Christianity

stories that occurred at particular times and in particular places.[1] Everything that gives the Judaic and Christian faiths their power is understood and remembered in relation to story. For Judaism, the story begins with a history of Abraham, Isaac, and Jacob, and carries on through centuries of trials, tribulations, and revelation. But this story of their history is not factual as we would think of history today. Rather, it is a metaphor for the Israelite's struggle to understand their one God, variously named Yahweh, Adonai, and Elohim. Christianity has carried on from that tradition. From its earliest stages, it has kept its connection with the down-to-earth history of Abraham, Isaac, and Jacob, and continues onwards using the metaphor of the birth, death, and resurrection of Jesus to convey the impact the actual Jesus had on his followers and the revelations about God he brought to the world. Biblical faith, therefore, takes the form of a "history."

So, just as it is true in the past, it is true today that the Jewish people and those of the Christian tradition are intimately connected. First, both Jews and Christians speak of God's covenants. The first covenant was with all humanity, through the mythological story of Noah: God promised never to wipe out the human race again. Subsequently, this first covenant of Noah evolved into the second one of Moses, often referred to by Christians as the old covenant. This Mosaic covenant expanded the Noah one by outlining rules and regulations, through the Ten Commandments, about exactly how God would fulfill his promise to Abraham.

The advent of Jesus ultimately created a third or new covenant, as claimed by Christians. The rewording of the Noah-Mosaic covenant was refined or updated to the golden-rule format: Love your neighbor as yourself.[2] This "new" covenant in Christianity does not replace or supersede God's covenant with the people of Israel; rather, it enlarges and fulfills the latter

---

1. Down-to-earth stories are not universal. Some forms of Greek and pagan philosophy, which arose more or less at the same time, chose to speak of human existence without reference to any concrete history. Instead, they preferred to focus on ideas or myths cast in a timeless eternity—not so with the biblical religions of Christianity and Judaism.

2. Post-modern Christianity begins to veer away here from traditional Christian dogma. Jesus was Jewish, a rabbi reformer. His primary focus was the synagogue and its emphasis on the letter of the law, rather than its spirit. Jesus did not bring a new covenant; he preached the original Mosaic covenant, albeit with a consciousness five hundred years more modern than that of the Moses tradition. Thus, his use of words and metaphors was different. The golden rule of "Love your neighbor as yourself" is quite implicit in Deuteronomy.

Why the Hebrew Scriptures?

amid the Gentiles. Likewise, the New Testament does not supplant God's original covenant but instead, extends God's promises to all of humanity.

Second, the other major parallel between Judaism and Christianity is that Judaism looks toward its "land of milk and honey," while Christianity looks to the "Kingdom of God," a new metaphor but the same God. The same intent pervades both faiths. Today, we might call this God-consciousness.[3]

Theologically, key differences between Jews and Christians seem inconsequential today. Jews attest their faith simply by being Jews. One enters into the Jewish community by being born into it. Christians are more like sojourners in history and strangers in every land, every social order. Although they may be citizens within various social orders and cultures, they do not see their fundamental identity before God as connected with land, place, or ethnicity, but with the faith of Abraham. One enters into the Christian community through faith.[4]

Every reenactment in Jewish and Christian worship retells the history of God's covenant people. Jews have three liturgical feasts or seasons—Passover, Tabernacles, and Weeks (Pesach, Sukkoth, Shabuoth)—which reflect the phases of revelation, redemption, and community-creation out of the Exodus-Wandering in the Wilderness story that brought the people of Israel into being. Christians similarly reenact the analogous seasons: the birth of Jesus (revelation), the resurrection (redemption), and Pentecost, the coming of the Holy Spirit (community-creation).

These reenactments are more accurately remembered as one history, not two. In the Passover Haggadic prayer, the Jew says, "All this I do because of what God did for me in bringing me out of Egypt." The Christian believer participates in the same history, viewed through the lens of the life of Jesus: "All this I do because of what God did for me in the coming of Jesus."

---

3. There are three faith traditions of the Book: Judaism, Christianity, and Islam. Islam shares this metaphor and calls it Paradise. All three metaphors refer, essentially, to the same state of consciousness.

4. Jesus, being Jewish, focused almost entirely on the Jewish community. After his execution, his followers (primarily Paul) began to face outwards spiritually towards the Gentiles. They began to bring others who were not *ethnically* sons of Abraham into the covenant of God with Israel by faith. By the time Jerusalem was destroyed, the Gentiles began to outnumber the Jews. The nature of the movement began to diverge from its Jewish roots and so emerged the Church.

Chapter 2

Why Post-modern Christianity?

CHRISTIANITY, WHETHER PRE-MODERN OR modern, holds its identity through Jesus Christ. But as already noted, the historical person, Jesus of Nazareth, was not a Christian. He did not even start Christianity. As an itinerate Jewish preacher, Jesus was unquestionably good at what he did. He was charismatic, he could heal, he walked his talk, and people recognized something special in him that we would call holy.[1]

He provoked the rich and powerful, confronting their self-declared importance and control over others. His challenge to the Jewish and Roman leadership grew to the point where the establishment felt it necessary to eliminate him to preserve their status quo. We know that most of his followers abandoned him when he was seized and executed (by crucifixion). We also know that after Jesus' death, they came back together because the spirit Jesus, so talked about and exemplified, seemed to still be around, stronger than ever. These followers continued Jesus' mission and their group grew rapidly. As mentioned earlier, they became a new Judaic sect known as The Way, adding to the other dozen or so sects that already existed.

These were turbulent times, however. The Romans destroyed Jerusalem around 70 CE (Christian or Common Era) and again a few years later. The Jewish people and their varied faith traditions[2] were scattered all around the Mediterranean. Unlike the more traditional Jewish sects, The

---

1. We believe that Jesus was truly a shaman who could heal. Shamans exist today. We do however have to recognize that several of the "miracle" stories (walking on water, turning water into wine, etc) are metaphor, not fact.

2. There was no single, uniform Hebrew religion at the time of Jesus. There were perhaps as many as a dozen versions of the religions that claimed Moses and the Torah. "The Way" was one of them. The term "Judaic" came into use only after several centuries.

Why Post-modern Christianity?

Way began attracting Gentiles. Soon, The Way became predominantly more Gentile than Jewish and evolved into what became known as Christianity.[3] But the church did not get off to an easy start because after the dispersal of the Jewish sects due to the Roman conquest of Jerusalem, The Way itself splintered into several factions, each with its own interpretation of Jesus' teachings and understanding of his crucifixion; was this event a miracle, vision, dream, or metaphor? This was no simple matter; the various sects had major, fundamental differences. This, naturally, led to much tumult and many exiles, political intrigues, and leaders rising, falling, and rising again. There were even assassinations amongst the groups—all in the name of God, of course. This also led to a proliferation of writings called gospels.

Ultimately, as might be expected, there were winners and losers. The winners were a group who tended to interpret narrowly the life of Jesus. They kept Christianity highly hierarchical, centered around leadership that claimed to have direct authority from God. They created an official creed and selected an official church reading list[4], which included only those writings that supported their point of view. Eventually, aligned with the establishment plus the government of Rome, this conservative group held a defining meeting at Nicaea, around 330 CE. A government-sanctioned *orthodox* Christianity was born.[5]

Today, as we know in the western and developing world, there is a multitude of varieties and sects within the Catholic and Protestant traditions. Yet, they mostly ascribe to a basic doctrine set out so many centuries ago: we are born with original sin, Jesus was the son of God (literally or at least, a special messenger sent by God), and the crucifixion of Jesus and his bodily resurrection were the vehicles through which people are "saved" from, or receive atonement from, their sin.[6] These were "facts" that people had to believe. For the most part, orthodox or western Christianity

---

3. What we know today as Judaism evolved as well, but that is another story.

4. Now known as the church canon.

5. This is not to be confused with the group called Eastern Orthodox churches, which are included under the umbrella of orthodox Christianity.

6. Most of this traditional Christian dogma stems directly from Jewish theology that was swirling around in that region at the time of Jesus. Some Jewish sects were expecting a divine messiah while other sects rejected this mythology. It was an active topic of debate. The divine messiah coming to earth as a man and then later being carried back up to heaven is believed by scholars to be a combination of two much older myths whose origins are unknown. Part of the myth attached to Jesus the teacher can be found in the book of Daniel. Jewish myth in general has largely been borrowed from the mythologies of several other societies.

remains heavily invested in dogma and strongly rooted in the church as an institution.

The losers did not fare so well. Their take on Jesus was egalitarian and spiritual and they emphasized inner knowledge rather than intellectual belief. Their path was known as Gnosticism.[7] Because it was relatively unstructured and had no rigid dogma, Gnosticism didn't have a chance against the government-sanctioned orthodox church. Declared heretical, the Gnostic churches were expelled. Their writings were banned and most were destroyed. A few, though, were hidden. Fortunately, some of these hidden collections were discovered around 1945 by accident in caves in an area of Egypt called Nag Hammadi. (These are not to be confused with the Dead Sea Scrolls, found at roughly the same time in what is now the West Bank.) Previously, modern scholars knew nothing of most of the Gnostic writings.

Unlike the orthodox Christians, the Gnostics interpreted the teachings of Jesus less literally. They believed that the Kingdom of Heaven was a state of awareness or consciousness inherent in everyone and could be realized by looking inward. In their view, judgment and forgiveness of sin were not things that a deity would do. Rather, sin—what we might call doing and thinking "bad" things—would naturally fade away as an individual's consciousness was raised. Theirs was a much more contemplative spiritual journey.

We may lament that official Christianity existed for about seventeen-hundred years without the insight of Gnosticism. Nevertheless, and in spite of the numberless atrocities and crimes committed in its name, Christianity has worked surprisingly well. It has had its mystics and has acknowledged the mystery of God. It has brought untold millions of people the love and comfort of God and is still doing so. But in the last sixty years or so, it has lost its impact on most in our society.

A major shakeup is happening within the Christian Church, however. It started in the 1800s with the advent of serious biblical criticism and has recently accelerated because of the uncovered wisdom of Gnosticism.

---

7. Gnosis derives from the Greek term for "knowing" as in "knowing yourself." The Gnostics were a very exclusive group with strict rules as to who the believers were. They lived in a rather extreme form of isolation, thinking of the physical world as intrinsically evil and, thus, rejecting all contact with the outside. That aside, their writings reflected a mystical or highly spiritual theology that we today call Gnosticism.

Many Christians have found that the church, with its continued archaic set of beliefs and creeds, is neglecting its historical roots with Judaism and with Jesus as a teacher. Without this foundation, it has wandered into areas of questionable integrity and theology such as intolerance, elitism, discrimination, and exclusiveness. The church has forgotten the origin and purpose of story, which was originally designed to express the mystery of God. The church turned story into literal-minded dogma and hence, cut off inquiry and seeking. It lost its way and relevance. Now it has been supplanted by the faith of unlimited consumerism and power, necessitating the rise of post-modern Christianity[8].

Many groups and schools of thought, of course, lay claim to the terms "emergent Christianity" or "post-modern Christianity." Unfortunately, progress in many churches involves so-called innovations like changing the arrangements of pews. Beneath such changes still lie the rigid creeds, structure, and authority. Nevertheless, serious writers and scholars, such as Walter Brueggemann, John Dominic Crossan, Brian McLaren, and Tony Jones, are examining a new Christianity. Their post-modern version refers to a movement that begins to recover the lost heritage of the Gnostics.

This movement breaks with current practices in two significant ways. First, post-modern Christianity returns to the very basics of Moses and Jesus yet acknowledges that their understanding of the cosmos was monumentally simpler than our awareness today. Without question, post-modern Christianity holds to the following: faith in the Creator and in the God of Abraham; a commitment to God's commandments; justice and mercy; a sense of contrition; and the sanctity of life. And it most definitely holds to the Jewish view that humankind's awareness of God evolved through history. It certainly recommits to the Hebrew Bible as a metaphorical story of a people's struggle to understand life and the spiritual force that we call God. This remains our mythology. It deepens Christianity, however, by venturing well beyond Christology (the singular worship of Jesus as God) and the preoccupation with the forgiveness of sin. Rather, post-modern Christianity looks intensely at mysticism of the Gnostics and at the Jesus of history, Jesus the Jew and rabbi, and Jesus of the Torah. To understand the Jesus

---

8. It is recognized that "post-modern" is a much used and vaguely defined term. In this book, post-modern is used to convey a sense of unease about many of the long-held assumptions and grand stories that underpin our society. Our society appears to be losing direction, our ways of thinking and understanding no longer seem adequate for a rapidly changing world. In order to cope we must question and de-construct the tenants by which our culture functions.

of history, we have to understand the two commandments that he reiterated from the more ancient Hebrew writings: (i) Love God with all your heart, mind, and strength (or Radically center yourselves in God) and (ii) Love your neighbor as yourself; participate in God's passion for a different kind of world, one marked by absolute justice, equality, and economics of abundance for all. This is the goal. It's that simple. We grow in these aims, not only through stories about Jesus of the Christian scriptures, but also through the study of the Hebrew scriptures, which gave Jesus the context for his ministry.

The second major change that post-modern Christianity brings to spirituality is a twenty-first-century understanding of "God." The vast majority of those of Judaic and Christian faith have traditionally considered God an actual player, an entity who takes action and intervenes in naturally occurring events. We ask God to do things for us. But our concept of God should evolve along with our understanding of the universe. Such evolution of understanding is apparent even in the Bible. We see how the concept of God changes from that of a deity that walks with you in the garden or calls upon someone to sacrifice their child (stories from Genesis) and becomes more and more abstract. We see that living covenant, God's vision, the Kingdom of Heaven, is truly a state of mind, a level of consciousness that transcends ego. Our post-modern understanding of God, therefore, removes the concept of God as judge or deity who gets angry or rewards behavior or has a will in the same way that we might will something to happen. Similarly, the status of "chosen people" no longer exists.[9] More simply put: God is and things happen. What becomes important is not what happens but rather, how we respond to it.[10]

9. The traditional Jewish story claims that God specifically chose to work with their nation over all other societies. The term "chosen people" arises time and time again in Deuteronomy, for example. Today, it forms the basis of Israel's claim to land in Palestine. One might wonder whether the Deuteronomists intended this term to be metaphorical or truly literal.

10 Taken further, we can talk about God not simply as the Creator, but as the underlying substance or sustainer of this universe and any others that we may care to contemplate. To put it another way, the time/space realm that we inhabit is, in itself, a manifestation of God. From this perspective, we ourselves are a product of time/space, thus a manifestation God "created in the image of God." (Being a manifestation of God is never to be confused with thinking that we are God. There's a huge difference.) To pursue this model, if we accept that our consciousness, through which we know good and evil, is also from beyond time/space, then we can say that our consciousness is the means by which the universe or time/space or God can observe or know itself. This view is an ancient Hindu teaching.

Why Post-modern Christianity?

We consider what we call God a force or presence, not an entity or deity. We experience this ever-present, ever-persistent force as love.[11] God is a lover. Lovers do not cause or prevent earthquakes or plagues or leukemia or stubbed toes. Rather, just as lovers help us deal with such afflictions, so does God, as ultimate love, absolute truth, and absolute justice. We cease to worship God, as though God needs an ego boost. We no longer believe in God. Instead, we open ourselves to this unknowable presence. We come to know God. And knowing God in our bones, so to speak, our life begins to change.

---

11. I use the term "experience" in the sense that we experience love. However, the deepest thoughts/intuitions of the Christian mystics are that this has little to do with experiences, as we normally define them today. Instead, it has much to do with an awareness of this "outside" permeating our "inside," not as an experience *per se* but as the "is" of existence.

Chapter 3

Background to Deuteronomy

As stated in Chapter 1, because Christianity arose from and is so deeply enmeshed in Judaism, we cannot fully understand it, particularly from a post-modern perspective, without the foundation of the Hebrew Scriptures. And Deuteronomy provides a direct path into the Judaic faith.

It is impossible to overstate the importance of the book of Deuteronomy in Israel's faith—it puts forth the very essence of Judaism (and, hence, much of Christianity). The book is about the covenant between Yahweh and Israel. Both pledge complete loyalty to each other: Yahweh is to assure the well-being of Israel and Israel is to live in trust in, and obedience of, Yahweh.

The book of Deuteronomy is organized into three great speeches of Moses—chapters 1 to 4, 4 to 28, and 29 to 32—with a concluding section that concerns the death of Moses, the leadership of Joshua, and the future of Israel. Most attention is given to the long, middle speech, which forms the bulk of the book. This is likely the oldest part of the book and contains materials gathered over a long period of time. This speech is the focus of this commentary.

The Context

The book of Deuteronomy is a metaphor. At the end of a long wilderness journey (the Exodus from Egypt), the Israelites prepare to cross the Jordan River to conquer the promised land, the land of milk and honey. The book is written as a series of addresses *by Moses* to Israel. Moses addresses Israel with a strong message about God's covenant, which is a simple either/or: either the people obey God's commands and prosper or they don't obey

Background to Deuteronomy

and will disappear. There is no mincing of words here. Moses knows the land of promise, which is not empty; it has long been settled by the Canaanites. Thus, even if the Israelites successfully conquer the land, they will find themselves in a serious fix. The seductive cultures and religions that already exist there will severely challenge their faith in Yahweh. They will always face a choice, every moment of every day: the easy path of giving in to pleasure and greed or the difficult one of obeying Yahweh. The latter choice just happens to be the only road to survival.

About Moses

There is little, if any, evidence that a person such as Moses ever existed. Rather, Moses was an ancient tradition dating back to the legends of Sinai, where the basics of Judaism are said to have originated. In this tradition, anything attributed to Moses was deemed authoritative. Therefore, the use of Moses in Deuteronomy was a deliberate device used by the authors to make an important claim.[1]

The Origins and Development

The origins of the materials in Deuteronomy are lost in the mists of time. Most likely, they come from all around the Mediterranean region over several centuries. The Hebrew people living in Canaan[2] collected the materials as part of their cultural identity. They were a living document intended to provide direction in response to various crises (primarily wars and exile) that threatened their society. Therefore, editing of the document was ongoing: old material was revised and new material incorporated as needed. This makes it hard to put a date on Deuteronomy's creation. The final

---

1. This fabrication is not a deception or intended to fool anyone, for the ancient world did not focus on precise personal authorship the way that we do today. This tradition continued in the Christian scriptures, whereby the gospels are attributed to Jesus' disciples, most of whom would have been long dead by the time the gospels, as we know them today, were written (the exception being Mark which is believed to have been written around 50CE.)

2. Don't get confused here. The Israelites were already indigenous to Canaan. But in securing their identity, they cobbled together this story of leaving Egypt *en masse*, wandering the wilderness for forty years, finally arriving at the Jordon, and getting ready to invade Canaan. Underlying this tale, of course, is the real story of their wrestling with God: their growing knowledge and conscious awareness of God.

written version was compiled most likely around 500 to 600 BCE during the Babylonian exile (another crisis).

The Setting

The "historical" setting of the book of Deuteronomy is roughly two hundred years before it was written, probably 700 to 600 BCE. This was a period when Canaan was dominated by one of many empires that rose and declined in that part of the world.

The Big Issue

The book represents a hard-fought consensus in Israel about the key claims of Yahwistic faith. As stated earlier, one key claim concerns the exclusive *gift* and *demand* of Yahweh: A prosperous life (the gift) comes only with loyalty to Yahweh (the demand), which has to be front and center in every aspect of life.

So, what is this community to look like? In the list of rules and regulations (chapters 12 to 25), we can see the attempt to state exactly what Yahweh's exclusive rule means. A Torah-based community is nothing less than radical. It is to take the form of (i) a "Sabbath economy," in which there is abundance for all (as opposed to the artificial economy of scarcity we have today) and a radical, absolutely just distribution of this abundance; (ii) a politics of discipline and compassion; and (iii) a faith that cedes all authority to the holy. It is to be a community of radical equality, viable public power, faithful conduct of war, and sustainable ordering of family life. It is to be a distinct community, a "contrast society," one that clearly shows that it is different from all others. The writers know that their proposed alternative way, based on complete consciousness of God, is their only option.

But this path was not so simple: The Israelites did not live that way. Like us today, they had egos,[3] which provided for cheating, lying, and stealing. Deuteronomy recognized this reality. Thus, in addition to describing God's dream for us, Deuteronomy has a second agenda—to describe how

---

3. I use the term "ego" as that with which we identify ourselves externally. We know good and evil because of our self-consciousness and most often choose to try to do good. Nevertheless, our egos also involve instincts to survive, propagate, and eat; these reside in our brain stems and without them, we would never have evolved. Hence, we still lust, have greed, and like to have power over others.

people live together while waiting for their consciousness to overcome their ego's need for power and acquisition.

We see this immediately when we study the laws. We can see a strong tension between considerable generosity among members of the community and harsh stands on anything that could cause social disorder in that community. As long as community members abide by common rules of behavior, there is generosity among them. However, if an individual or family acts contrary to the common good, there are strict punishments. Similarly, since Israel does not exist in a vacuum, Deuteronomy must struggle with the difficult issue of who is in and who is out. There is a generosity to foreigners but only if there aren't many of them. There is deep anxiety about keeping people from other cultures out in order to maintain the community. Israel is *in* the world ("in Canaan") but not *of* the world ("Canaanite"). Some responses to this issue are clumsy and awkward, but the issue is, for that reason, no less important. So, without any attempt to "explain away" the harshness in the text, we can see that the harshness reflects high anxiety.

Despite this tension, however, we see that Deuteronomy set in motion not only the goal of achieving oneness with God but also an ethic that still continues today in the revolutionary ethical convictions of Judaism and Christianity.

Its Relevance Today

Perhaps one of the most outstanding things about Deuteronomy is that it demands that *the Torah be stated in fresh ways for each generation*. Time and again, phrases warn against literalism. In other words, a fixed interpretation was never intended. Even today, in the light of new circumstances, the content always remains open to being revisited and reinterpreted. We must allow Deuteronomy to be a metaphor, a use of words *other than in their literal sense*. Such awareness does not give license for the text to mean just anything. Instead, it means: Listen attentively for what may be present in the text beyond what is obvious.

The theological point of this text, then, is a sense that the community must *always* redefine itself in terms of its origin, purpose, and destiny. The land may then be understood as hope for the promised well-being that comes later to be called the Kingdom of God. In Deuteronomy, Israel is not yet in the land—it is on the way there. How it gets there is the overriding issue. It takes Moses to insist that this covenant community, responsive only to Yahweh, understands the terms upon which its future depends. Moses knows that the future is a gift, but one that can be readily lost. Israel must always re-choose that future in the form of obedience in the present. No wonder the book of Deuteronomy worries about children; the future is always the task of the next generation, which, hopefully, has listened long and well enough to choose wisely.[4]

The real choice offered Israel is a covenant or idols. And we are offered the same choice today, perhaps even more urgently. As Jews and Christians, we can choose covenant, a life totally devoted to enacting God's dream for us, or we can choose idols, the power of commodities and the laws of commerce which, to the same degree, command complete loyalty and have complete authority. As much as we might wish, there is no happy medium, no compromise.[5]

Thus, it is not a big move from the warning of Moses to our present context. At that ancient boundary, Moses understood that the ethical stakes in a decision for Torah were very high. They continue to be very

---

4. A thousand years later, the same message from Jesus was still as relevant and urgent. Today, the message to us in the church and from us to the world is no less relevant and urgent. We may take land as a metaphor for a viable communal existence that protects and enhances a shared humanity.

5. We have already chosen because we are totally immersed in a culture that has us behave as nothing more than a consumer unit. Our individuality has become a commodity, used by the powerful and wealthy for their exclusive benefit. Now, we may engage in some dialogue to counter the consumer-unit idol. Faith traditions may try to preach against it, but on the whole, churches and temples in North America buy into the consumer culture. It might be a slightly softer, more humanitarian culture, but a consumer-unit culture nevertheless.

Predominant culture is very difficult to counter. It is so much easier to give up and be carried along by the continually renewed wave of images generated by the secular culture. These images of so-called happiness are of buying a new car or having whiter teeth or rooting for the winning team or making lots of money or committing adultery or having a high-prestige job or living in the right area and drinking expensive scotch. Even worse is giving into the humanitarian consumer-unit image, e.g., contributing to a food bank or housing the homeless rather than forcing our society to change the economics that create homelessness and the need for food banks.

Images are essential if we are to avoid seeing the day-to-day reality in which we live. To live without images, to face the world as it truly is, would only make us more conscious of our emptiness and impotence and the insignificance of our situation. With advertising images, however, everything unpleasant is erased and our drab existence decorated by their charm and sparkle. Since, above all, we must not become aware of reality, images create a substitute reality. Artificial images, passing themselves off as truth, erase the reality of our life and society.

Background to Deuteronomy

high. Choosing covenant with all its prerequisites, perplexity, and exposition was not easy then. Nor is it now.

Let's put it another way. As Christians, we might easily slip into a comfortable complacency. Yes, through Jesus' death and resurrection, we have our sins forgiven, but when this becomes too literal, is this not just one more image, a passing-the-buck, so to speak? Explanations like "God is in command" or "I try to do God's will" can become an almost immoral interpretation of Jesus, allowing us to avoid a personal and social covenant with God, who requires us to create a society of distributive justice, an alternative reality that Deuteronomy lays out so clearly.

The Language of Commentary

There is one more housekeeping issue and that concerns language. Postmodern commentary on anything biblical is in its infancy and the related language that we use has not fully developed. In some ways, traditional language is defective, yet that is often all that we have readily available and familiar. This might seem contradictory. For instance, early in this commentary, you will come across the issue of tributes made to Yahweh and Yahweh returning them because Yahweh doesn't need them. Obviously, this needs to be radically reinterpreted or, indeed, replaced if we are to mature in our theological outlook. The absolute or the love force that we call God does not need tributes. Nonetheless, post-modern Christians honor and revere God as deeply as anyone else, and worship in whatever form is natural and necessary. Tradition and metaphor are not eliminated by any means. We are talking here of concept, of understanding, that may increase our intimacy with that which we call God. This has nothing to do with our experience of God or how we approach God personally.

So, with that background, we head into the text itself.

We don't start with chapter 1 verse 1. As mentioned, Deuteronomy has three sections, the middle one believed to being the oldest. The first and third are later add-ons. We will focus here on the middle section, which begins with chapter 4, verse 44. This is the second speech of Moses. It accounts for the major material of Deuteronomy and constitutes its essential teaching.

Chapter 4

The Setting and the Basics

Deut 4: 44–49
The Boundary of Decision-making

> *This is the law that Moses set before the Israelites. ₄₅ These are the decrees and the statutes and ordinances that Moses spoke to the Israelites when they had come out of Egypt, ₄₆ beyond the Jordan in the valley opposite Beth-peor, in the land of King Sihon of the Amorites, who reigned at Heshbon, whom Moses and the Israelites defeated when they came out of Egypt. ₄₇ They occupied his land and the land of King Og of Bashan, the two kings of the Amorites on the eastern side of the Jordan: ₄₈ from Aroer, which is on the edge of the Wadi Arnon, as far as Mount Sirion (that is, Hermon), ₄₉ together with all the Arabah on the east side of the Jordan as far as the Sea of the Arabah, under the slopes of Pisgah.*[1]

Israel is at the *boundary of decision-making*. These few verses ground the speech, so to speak, to a specific time and place, emphasizing the tradition of basing Israel's story on aspects of true history.[2] Keep in mind the tribal nature of the society at that time and its attachment to place. True, there may be some actual historical memory in these traditions but little or no archeological evidence exists, to date, of an exodus or conquering of

---

1. All scripture excerpts are from the New Revised Standard Version Bible, copyright 1989, division of Christian Education of the National Council of the Churches of Christ in the U.S.

2. Remember: This is all story, not what we would today call factual. Its uniqueness as mythology lies in its apparent reality as opposed to equivalent stories from Greek or Hindu mythology.

The Setting and the Basics

a foreign land. Research indicates that Israelite society evolved gradually from within an already settled region. Of course, this has no bearing on the importance of the "boundary of decision-making." As already stated, Israel was always reaching such boundaries (or, the opportunity for change was always presenting itself). This is still happening to us and the synagogue, church, and temple today.

Deut 5: 1–5
Hear God

> *Moses convened all Israel, and said to them: Hear, O Israel, the statutes and ordinances that I am addressing to you today; you shall learn them and observe them diligently. ₂ The Lord our God made a covenant with us at Horeb. ₃ Not with our ancestors did the Lord make this covenant, but with us, who are all of us here alive today. ₄ The Lord spoke with you face to face at the mountain, out of the fire. ₅ (At that time I was standing between the Lord and you to declare to you the words of the Lord; for you were afraid because of the fire and did not go up the mountain.)*

The first word is "Hear." In other words, stop chattering. Stop restless activity. Stop your current life for once . . . and just listen . . . Hear God.

Of course there is a dilemma with an "historical" tradition. If a covenant was given several generations ago, the current generation might think that it no longer applies. Deuteronomy has to make the past become the present. The words of Moses address *what has already happened* but Moses emphasizes that the covenant is *here and now*, not *there and then*.

Deut 5: 6–10
The Ten Commandments—Part 1—Honor God

> *And he said: ₆ I am the Lord your God, who brought you out of the land of Egypt, out of the house of slavery; ₇ you shall have no other gods before me. ₈ You shall not make for yourself an idol, whether in the form of anything that is in heaven above, or that is on the earth beneath, or that is in the water under the earth. ₉ You shall not bow down to them or worship them; for I the Lord your God am a jealous God, punishing children for the iniquity of parents, to the third and fourth generation of those who reject me, ₁₀ but showing steadfast*

> *love to the thousandth generation of those who love me and keep my commandments.*

Moses now begins God's most basic demands. Verses 6–7 are the crux of the scriptures. They say it all: "You shall have no other gods before me"—not the god of wealth or power or status or pride or self. This is the God who allowed for the exodus and who continues to bring further exoduses (verse 6) or boundaries of decision-making. During the exodus, the pharaoh is displaced and Yahweh becomes the new lord and master of Israel. The God who has liberated Israel now issues commands about the future, how Israel is to create a just society.

In the simple language of verses 7 to 11, God is shown to be way beyond Israel in majesty, power, and authority. Essentially, God is beyond humankind's wildest imagination. This is a new concept. Yahweh is outside any normal categories of religion. And so, Israel has to recognize God and deal with God differently than ever before. The commands clearly do away with any *familiarity with, or presumption about,* Yahweh.[3] The very name Yahweh is intended to be unpronounceable; how could someone think that he or she could truly put a name to God? God is massively powerful but also very concerned for the lowly slave. Unquestionably, God is much involved in everyday social and economic matters and will not share power at all with the pharaoh or any other would-be sovereign, including the pharaoh of commodity and ownership. Yahweh is irreversibly on the side of liberation. A covenant-based society governed by Yahweh's rule will be a society that overcomes oppression and exploitation.[4]

This has to be emphasized. Unlike any of the other gods available, this God claims undivided loyalty, undivided consciousness. The relationship between Yahweh and the Israelites must be exclusive. It depends on willing, glad loyalty. But this loyalty to Yahweh is different from the loyalty

---

3. It is not possible to trace any specific development in the history of religion for this claim of Yahweh. There is concrete evidence of a gradual formation or slow realization about the single, all-powerful nature of God. This concept shows its head here and there, primarily in Egypt, in some very early scraps of writing. Then again, in Genesis, there are still remnants of several gods. However, in Deuteronomy, it appears as a given. The power and influence of this insight on our distant ancestors cannot be overemphasized.

4. In today's terms, we can say that the spirit force that we call God is massively powerful. Those who truly are receptive to it have no choice but to be concerned for the lowly, the outcast, and the poor. Those who allow this life-changing influence into their lives are intimately involved in everyday social and economic matters. This drive is well beyond will, it is a naturally occurring outcome of "knowing God."

The Setting and the Basics

previously demanded by the pharaoh. Earthly rulers say: "Be loyal or die." God is saying: "Be loyal and thrive." This is a two-way relationship, one that is all-demanding but also all-giving.

Unlike the other gods, this God refuses any religious form (verses 8–10). The prohibition against images safeguards the freedom of Yahweh to be fully relational and fully involved in life, but not limited, of course, by life or by humans trying to describe God or God's will. Any attempt to define or limit Yahweh is prohibited. These commands say that God cannot be tamed. It is prohibited! This statement is as true today as it was then.

Deut 5: 11
Revere Yahweh

You shall not make wrongful use of the name of the Lord your God, for the Lord will not acquit anyone who misuses his name.

Contrary to common interpretation, this is not about cursing or bad language. Rather, it resists use of Yahweh's power, authority, or reputation for any causes—political, economic, moral or ecclesial. Unlike other gods available, this is not a god who lends God's name to any earthly cause. No nation, team or other group can say that God is on its side in a struggle. Yahweh is not "useful"; Yahweh has no utilitarian value. This God will be worshiped only for the sake of Yahweh's own life, purpose, and way in the world. The wrong use of Yahweh's name seeks to draw Yahweh's power into more frivolous modes of life where human beings retain control. Instead, Yahweh is to be revered, not to be put to use in any way.

Deut 5: 12–15
The Ten Commandments—Part 2—Observe the Sabbath

Observe the Sabbath day and keep it holy, as the Lord your God commanded you. $_{13}$ Six days you shall labor and do all your work. $_{14}$ But the seventh day is a Sabbath to the Lord your God; you shall not do any work—you, or your son or your daughter, or your male or female slave, or your ox or your donkey, or any of your livestock, or the resident alien in your towns, so that your male and female slave may rest as well as you. $_{15}$ Remember that you were a slave in the land of Egypt, and the Lord your God brought you out from there

Deuteronomy and Post-Modern Christianity

> *with a mighty hand and an outstretched arm; therefore the Lord your God commanded you to keep the Sabbath day.*

Addressed to a community facing a life-or-death decision, Deuteronomy is concerned that Israel should re-choose its own distinctive identity as the people of Yahweh. That depends, in part, on thinking differently. It also requires visible practices that the young of the community and non-Israelites can see publicly. By the sixth century BCE, the Deuteronomic tradition emphasized the Sabbath as a visible, concrete difference. Today, we cannot overemphasize the importance of this act, keeping the following in mind:

- The Sabbath is a courageous *public act of identity*. On this day, Israelites act differently from any other group of people. Others see them acting differently and they see each other acting differently. This difference is economic, of course, but it is also highly theological. This rest is one that slaves have never enjoyed before, a rest now available because Yahweh was then, and is, always engaged in breaking the coercions of slavery.

- The Sabbath is an *act of resistance*. The key characteristic of the day is not worship but rest. It is work stoppage. And in that work stoppage, Israel states that it does not belong to, and is not defined by, the production pressures, schedules, and quotas of the world. Israel refuses to be defined by production (and consumption).

- The Sabbath is an occasion for *alternative community*. This is particularly evident in the final phrase of verse 14: your servant shall rest "as you." In any ordinary community, important social distinctions are related to power and privilege. Some rest while others work. This command says that on this day of work stoppage, all such distinctions are gone. The Sabbath overcomes social distinctions when slaves participate with masters in a world guaranteed by this free gift from God. This generosity extends in the community from the powerful to the powerless; the bank president and the dumpster-diver are equal in the "eyes" of God. It also extends from the insider to the outsider. The injunction of 1:16 had already insisted that "aliens" be included in covenantal justice; the resident alien is invited to the work stoppage as well. One day out of the week, aliens have no need to justify their presence in the community by productivity.

- The invention of Sabbath was, in its own way, the start of the environmental movement. The work stoppage, which included not only all members of the human community (masters and slaves, insiders and outsiders) but also non-human creatures (donkeys and livestock), indicated a sense that freedom under God included all of the environment, a recognition that even led to resting the land also in the Jubilee year.[5] (See Exodus 10:26.)

- The Sabbath is *an act of hope*. It is revolutionary and subverts established hierarchical society. It is a command that means that production is subordinate to the well-being of all humans, in contrast to a market economy or state socialism in which people exist solely for the sake of the economy (see Mark 2:27-28). This act of hope is indeed a visionary one in which the community is invited to dream of an ultimate alterative. The command "Rest" sets in motion a vision of an alternative society.

As mentioned earlier, Deuteronomy did not intend that the words of Moses be taken literally. This particular command is ripe for misinterpretation, though, and indeed it was. It did not take long before many rules were established regarding what was, and was not, permitted on the Sabbath. We see that clearly in the Christian scriptures when Jesus and his group were criticized about gathering some food to eat on the Sabbath. Jesus replied: *Don't misunderstand why I have come. I did not come to abolish the law of Moses or the writings of the prophets. No, I came to accomplish their purpose.* Matt 5: 7 (NLT 2007)

The point is that it is much easier to obey the letter of the law than the spirit behind it. For instance, I can certainly allow my staff to do no work on whatever day is my sabbath but ensure that they work extra hard on work days so that my profits do not suffer. That is not accomplishing the law's purpose.

---

5. Every seventh day is the Sabbath day, every seventh year, the Sabbath year. During the Sabbath year, the land is to lie fallow (at rest) and slaves are to be freed. Every seventh Sabbath year (forty-nine years) is called the Jubilee year. During this period, the land is not only to lie fallow, it is returned to the original owner, regardless of any other conditions. Through this tradition, no one can claim permanent control over large tracts of land nor can anyone become permanently homeless. This tradition might have evolved from an earlier Mesopotamian tradition.

Deuteronomy and Post-Modern Christianity

Deut 5: 16
The Ten Commandments—Part 3—Honor Your Parents

Honor your father and your mother, as the Lord your God commanded you, so that your days may be long and that it may go well with you in the land that the Lord your God is giving you.

The commandment to honor one's aging parents is closely related to the Sabbath. It, too, insists that human worth cannot be measured in terms of economic productivity. Parents who are no longer productive are indeed special candidates for Sabbath, endlessly at rest. As the sabbath command sweepingly celebrates *life beyond productivity,* the command about parents clearly states the ways in which society is to treat *those no longer productive.* This command is about social relationships—they are not to be grounded in utility. Deuteronomy and the entire covenantal tradition say that all social relationships are intrinsically valuable, without respect to utility.

The commandment in verse 16 invites reflection upon the fullest, richest notion of "family values." It is unfortunate that in recent time, "family values" have been reduced to a simplistic slogan that ignores the real issues of power and powerlessness. This commandment is not about having power over someone or about obedience. Indeed, it is quite the opposite. It simply reiterates the theme that all human beings are equal in the eyes of others, as they are in the eyes of God.

Further, this commandment is not intended to gloss over the fact that some parents have been, and continue to be, dysfunctional, badly abusing or neglecting their children. Adult children may have legitimate reasons to hate or reject their parent(s). It is indeed difficult to honor a parent who has abused or raped you. And yet, this parent is in the image of God, or created by God, or of God—a dilemma of faith-shattering dimensions. The adult child needs healing, which might become a lifelong process. In all likelihood, it will require coming to grips, in one form or another, with what his or her parent has done. The process of the victim learning, once again, to honor him or herself may, in some way, be an implicit (and most probably an unacknowledged) search for God in the parent.

Deut 5: 17–21
The Ten Commandments—Part 4—You Shall Not

You shall not murder. 18 Neither shall you commit adultery. 19 Neither shall you steal. 20 Neither shall you bear false witness against your neighbor. 21 Neither shall you covet your neighbor's wife. Neither shall you desire your neighbor's house, or field, or male or female slave, or ox, or donkey, or anything that belongs to your neighbor.

The series of five commands brings every zone of communal life under the rule of Yahweh. In each case, the prohibition curbs freedom of action that could be undertaken if the person were autonomous. The point of each command is that no one is independent under God. Each of us must live responsibly in the presence of our neighbor. The One who issues these commands is the One who insists that our independence must be limited by the reality of the neighbor whose entitlements are guaranteed by Yahweh.

1. In verse 17, the very life of the neighbor is held dear, protected, and guaranteed.

2. In verse 18, the dignity of the spouse is guaranteed by banning self-serving sexual satisfaction outside the marriage. Although an earlier, patriarchal version of the ban applied only to women, the man could do as he pleased. This later, more developed version prohibits both partners in a marriage from any external affairs. The seriousness with which these matters were regarded is shown by the harsh provisions of 22:13–30. Today, divorce is common, perhaps not as devastating to the family as it was then. At that time, society essentially expelled an abandoned or shamed woman (and her children) and they could easily starve or face extreme exploitation. God says: "No, no, we are all precious."

3. In verse 19, the property of the neighbor is protected against violent or secret confiscation. This is the beginning of the rule of law, which protects all, regardless of wealth.

4. Verse 20 expressly concerns the neighbor. This law recognizes that a viable society must have a reliable judiciary, so that members of the community have confidence in a fair hearing and settlement of claims. When truth-telling is compromised, society will revert to barbarism.

5. Verse 21: It has long been thought that "coveting" in the last commandment concerns envy. But more likely, the command concerns the practices of a society based on greed, in which the seizure of what belongs to a neighbor (a life, a spouse, any property or exploitation of the person's labor) is fair game for the clever against the slow, for the strong against the weak.

Recognizing that the neighbor's claim is central to each of these last five commands underscores their crucial importance. Think for a moment about the alternative: complete autonomy of each against all. Without legal, moral, covenantal restraint, the life, family, and property of each are at risk. Such an environment of greed and violence would (and does) make human community impossible or requires heavy imposition of the powerful over the powerless. Again, back to the main theme: All are valuable and equal under God. The law, thus, addresses not simply attitude. It also prevents the all-too-common practices and policies upheld by carefully arranged laws, whereby the weak are made defenseless.

The Deuteronomists saw that it was urgent for the community to return to an ethical vision—to recapture a sense of God's dream for them. They knew that a life committed only to productivity and money was, indeed, a recipe for death. They also knew that change would not happen by the mere use of old codes or rules. It could only happen by a change in their thinking and consciousness. Therefore, it becomes evident that the Ten Commandments were not simple moralisms or a series of virtues to be embraced. They were not simply ten rules to live by.[6] Yes, they are that, but taken all together, they become a sketch of a radical, alternative way of living in the world. The covenant shows a connectedness that changes everything. It demands an alternative community that lives differently every day.[7] It means one and all in the community must aim towards living the

---

6. Some scholars argue that the Ten Commandments were never intended to be rules, as such. Rather, they are the naturally occurring outcomes of a society that truly lives its vision of union with God. People living in true God-consciousness cannot help but recognize that each soul is of God and must be revered. The commandments of God have nothing to do with rules or our willpower. They have only to do with our seeking God.

7. Interestingly, five hundred years later, Jesus said exactly the same things as Moses. Jesus did not abolish the commandments; he came to complete them. Thus, in the Sermon on the Mount, the "new teaching" of Jesus affirms the old commandments and

Golden Rule, that is, loving their neighbor as themselves—as Jesus so succinctly put it. Obedience to the requirements of the holy God means giving up the treasures of self and replacing them with the neighborly rule of God.

This demand of Moses at the Jordan (and the demand of Jesus on the Mount) is still just as urgent today. We see our society as fragmented, broken, as "everyone for themselves." We see poverty and extreme wealth, pollution, corruption, anger, addictions. The demand of Moses, Jesus, and God is costly too. The costs and requirements of a just, truly sustainable community are very high. A genuinely human life is expensive because it gives up greed and self-centeredness. There is no place for "me" where the "me" does not live in total communion with God. Therefore, Moses has uttered the simplest, but most profound and urgent conditions for life. No amount of cleverness, technology, or arrogance can ever circumvent these terms of well-being.

The Ten Commandments, of course, are completely non-negotiable for Israel. But there is some irony here: they are endlessly negotiated. They must be interpreted to determine, time after time, that the command means this rather than that. Interestingly, they are such simple commands, so absolute, and yet, they require an active, ongoing discussion with God. One almost always has to ask "What is the precise meaning of this commandment?" within the lively engagement between Yahweh's will and day-to-day, real circumstance. Israel must continuously choose to return to its identity as Yahweh's people, and we must also do so today. Hence, the primary authority of the Decalogue (Ten Commandments) remains undoubted but their application to concrete circumstances is always an unfinished task. This means that as absolute as the commandments are, more must always be said. Within Judaism and Christianity, it is clear that discernment and interpretation will always continue. Any literalism that seeks to stop ongoing interpretation is alien to the tradition of Deuteronomy (and all scriptures, for that matter).

---

makes them more radical (Matt 5:17–48). Jesus aimed to regenerate a contrast society that embraced the commands in their greatest radicalism. It becomes clear that Jesus' exposition was, once again, a practical envisioning of how life may be lived in a world where God governs. Jesus is as clear as Moses on this one.

Chapter 5

Whys and Wherefores

Deut 5: 22–33
Moses is the Authority

These words the Lord spoke with a loud voice to your whole assembly at the mountain, out of the fire, the cloud, and the thick darkness, and he added no more. He wrote them on two stone tablets, and gave them to me. $_{23}$ When you heard the voice out of the darkness, while the mountain was burning with fire, you approached me, all the heads of your tribes and your elders; $_{24}$ and you said, "Look, the Lord our God has shown us his glory and greatness, and we have heard his voice out of the fire. Today we have seen that God may speak to someone and the person may still live. $_{25}$ So now why should we die? For this great fire will consume us; if we hear the voice of the Lord our God any longer, we shall die. $_{26}$ For who is there of all flesh that has heard the voice of the living God speaking out of fire, as we have, and remained alive? $_{27}$ Go near, you yourself, and hear all that the Lord our God will say. Then tell us everything that the Lord our God tells you, and we will listen and do it." $_{28}$ The Lord heard your words when you spoke to me, and the Lord said to me: "I have heard the words of this people, which they have spoken to you; they are right in all that they have spoken. $_{29}$ If only they had such a mind as this, to fear me and to keep all my commandments always, so that it might go well with them and with their children forever! $_{30}$ Go say to them, 'Return to your tents.' $_{31}$ But you, stand here by me, and I will tell you all the commandments, the statutes and the ordinances, that you shall teach them, so that they may do them in the land that I am giving them to possess." $_{32}$ You must therefore be careful to do as the Lord your God has commanded you; you shall not turn to *the right or to the left. ₃₃ You must follow exactly the path that the Lord your God has commanded you, so that you may live, and that it may go well with you, and that you may live long in the land that you are to possess.*

These remaining verses in chapter 5 set up Moses as the authority and the arbiter over the statutes and ordinances still to come.

At the time Deuteronomy was written, a well established tradition in Israel held that new prophesies and commands had to be based on earlier ones; there had to be a connection to the past. As mentioned earlier, whether Moses truly existed or not is not crucial. But the name Moses indicated a strong authority. Thus, the writers of Deuteronomy put their thinking into the form of a speech by Moses. The story in Exodus of Moses directly receiving the Ten Commandments from God was probably well known in the oral tradition of the tribes. Having Moses repeat them in Deuteronomy would not raise eyebrows. The authors had a larger agenda. Consider the Ten Commandments as policy statements. Every new situation that arose required a new interpretation of the commandments. A series of rules and regulations, at whatever stage of Israel's history, were never new but instead, developments from a past series. The name Moses, which provided the needed authority, ties the different series together.

The rules and regulations are still to come in chapters 12 to 25 but, first, chapters 6 to 11 set the background for these. Chapters 6 to 11 are the richest instructional and theological materials in the book of Deuteronomy, for they state the historical memories and motivations that give context to the commandments to follow.

Deut 6: 1–9
Show Total Commitment with Love

Now this is the commandment—the statutes and the ordinances—that the Lord your God charged me to teach you to observe in the land that you are about to cross into and occupy, ₂ so that you and your children and your children's children may fear the Lord your God all the days of your life, and keep all his decrees and his commandments that I am commanding you, so that your days may be long. ₃ Hear therefore, O Israel, and observe them diligently, so that it may go well with you, and so that you may multiply greatly in a land flowing with milk and honey, as the Lord, the God of your ancestors,

> has promised you. ₄ Hear, O Israel: The Lord is our God, the Lord alone. ₅ You shall love the Lord your God with all your heart, and with all your soul, and with all your might. ₆ Keep these words that I am commanding you today in your heart. ₇ Recite them to your children and talk about them when you are at home and when you are away, when you lie down and when you rise. ₈ Bind them as a sign on your hand, fix them as an emblem on your forehead, ₉ and write them on the doorposts of your house and on your gates.

The first nine verses of this chapter start the process of writing the commandments into everyone's memory. The covenant is total and it is radical. We have it again in verses 4–5, restated perhaps, but just as clear and hard-nosed as ever. This is the pivotal command of the entire tradition of Deuteronomy. It is impossible to overstate the importance of this summons. Faithful Jews recite these two verses daily; thus, some call them "the Jewish creed." In the teachings of Jesus, they are reckoned to be the first commandment.

The degree of total commitment required by Israel is expressed through the word "love." The term here is not a feeling or even an aptitude, but rather, a state of consciousness: love is comprised of naturally occurring, practical acts of obedience in every sphere of daily life. Israel will be totally, exclusively, without reservation, devoted to Yahweh in the world. Nothing less than that is commanded.

Community members have to imprint these commands in their minds because they are the distinguishing feature of the community. Loss of this memory will mean the loss of the community and that cannot be allowed. The tradition knows that if the commands are not obeyed, the land will revert to its anti-covenantal condition of exploitation. Israel, as a social experiment in the world, will evaporate before the forces of greed and anxiety. Therefore, Deuteronomy always has its eyes on the children. The command to hear is to be kept "in your heart," that is, at the center of one's sense of self. And if kept so focally, it will be effectively transmitted to the children, the coming generation. Moses proposes "saturation education" so that a child's imaginative horizon is completely pervaded by signs and reminders of this imperative. [1]

---

1. It is interesting to note that because of verses 8–9, most observant Jews have a scroll on their front door. Some strongly orthodox Jews wear a small box on their forehead, as a constant reminder.

Deut 6: 10–19
Develop Total Obedience to God

When the Lord your God has brought you into the land that he swore to your ancestors, to Abraham, to Isaac, and to Jacob, to give you a land with fine, large cities that you did not build, ₁₁ houses filled with all sorts of goods that you did not fill, hewn cisterns that you did not hew, vineyards and olive groves that you did not plant—and when you have eaten your fill, ₁₂ take care that you do not forget the Lord, who brought you out of the land of Egypt, out of the house of slavery. ₁₃ The Lord your God you shall fear; him you shall serve, and by his name alone you shall swear. ₁₄ Do not follow other gods, any of the gods of the peoples who are all around you, ₁₅ because the Lord your God, who is present with you, is a jealous God. The anger of the Lord your God would be kindled against you and he would destroy you from the face of the earth. ₁₆ Do not put the Lord your God to the test, as you tested him at Massah. ₁₇ You must diligently keep the commandments of the Lord your God, and his decrees, and his statutes that he has commanded you. ₁₈ Do what is right and good in the sight of the Lord, so that it may go well with you, and so that you may go in and occupy the good land that the Lord swore to your ancestors to give you, ₁₉ thrusting out all your enemies from before you, as the Lord has promised.

The demand for radical, exclusive obedience (verses 1–9) leads to a warning about disobedience (verses 10–19). This story takes place at the Jordan River; Israel is still in the wilderness where life-support systems are few. But Moses looks across the Jordan. There, he sees a future for Israel that is ripe for disobedience, for the good land of promise stands in contrast, in every way, to the present wilderness (verses 10–12). The coming land, the one promised since Genesis, offers everything a displaced people might want for well-being and security: cities, houses, cisterns, vineyards, groves, all the signs of blessedness and measures of prosperity. The cities are "great and good," the houses full, everything is in abundance. All these props for well-being, moreover, are a pure gift. Israel did nothing to achieve them, did not build, fill, hew, or plant. Everything is the gift of Yahweh, who gives in abundance. However, there is a "but."

Only in verse 12 does one arrive at the main verb of the sentence: "Take care." Pay attention! Unearned gifts can lead to satiation, which Moses knows produces amnesia. Amnesia is the great threat to a community whose defining relationship with God is grounded in a concrete memory.

Satiation banishes the past and obliterates the future. Everything is reduced to an endless present tense, rather like the absence of clocks in the casinos of Las Vegas. No one knows any longer what time it is, and no one can recall a time other than this one. It appears to be without beginning and end. In a state of satiation, Israel will lust after the gift but be uninterested in the giver. Israel will be tempted to forget the Exodus, will forget slavery, and the wondrous act of deliverance from slavery. Yahweh will no longer be remembered or known as the God of transformation; the distinctiveness of Yahweh and Yahweh's dream for people will evaporate into the gods of mindless consumption.

Today, verse 15 ("[T]he Lord your God . . . would destroy you from the face of the earth") is often interpreted as the other side of the covenant, a two-way deal like the covenant with the pharaoh: "Obey or die." But it is not truly a two-way deal; it is one-way, from God. God only gives. It is up to the people and individual to accept the gift or not. If people develop total obedience to God, they will receive the metaphorical land of milk and honey, a life of blessings beyond what they could ask or imagine. This is a free gift without strings. If they choose not to obey, if we choose not to open ourselves to the spirit of God, God is not going to do anything. The Spirit will not affect us. Life will carry on as before, with greed, violence, poverty, and oppression. Israel will be like any other nation, and we today will be like Israel, subject to the whims of power, satiated with goods, and under the tyranny of the consumer-military autocracy.

Deut 6: 20–25
Observe All These Statutes

When your children ask you in time to come, "What is the meaning of the decrees and the statutes and the ordinances that the Lord our God has commanded you?" $_{21}$ then you shall say to your children, "We were Pharaoh's slaves in Egypt, but the Lord brought us out of Egypt with a mighty hand. $_{22}$ The Lord displayed before our eyes great and awesome signs and wonders against Egypt, against Pharaoh and all his household. $_{23}$ He brought us out from there in order to bring us in, to give us the land that he promised on oath to our ancestors. $_{24}$ Then the Lord commanded us to observe all these statutes, to fear the Lord our God, for our lasting good, so as to keep us alive, as is now the case. $_{25}$ If we diligently observe this entire *commandment before the Lord our God, as he has commanded us, we will be in the right."*

The text returns to a focus on the children. Already, verse 2 affirmed that the obedience of the parents is necessary so that the children will fear and obey Yahweh. Living the faith itself is a way to nurture children and get them to ask questions about faith so that they can be taught it. We have to note that the word "fear" once meant awe and reverence; it did not mean today's more common usage of being afraid or anxious.

Reflection upon Moses's demand invites the following thoughts:

From the start, Deuteronomy raises two issues. The first concerns the survival of Israel as a nation. When Deuteronomy was written around 500 BCE, the Israelites were fighting for their survival as a nation in exile. They turned to the uniqueness of their god Yahweh and their loyalty to this *one* God. The stakes were high. Therefore, the idea of the jealous God in Deuteronomy is not about cosmic crankiness. Nor should we dismiss the language about the nation being wiped from the earth. This language is about the urgency of their situation, the importance of their taking on a radical, anti-imperialist identity. And they used the traditional authority, ascribed to Moses, to state their cause.

The second issue raised in Deuteronomy requires that we look at the story of Moses at a deeper level. The Israelites had to take on a new identity to survive. Fine. But the identity they chose just happened to be the most costly, most difficult one that any individual or group could ever attempt. The radical, anti-imperialist identity revolved around their dream of an ideal society. Their vision was a society in which everyone loved their neighbor as themselves. They knew that such a vision could happen only through unconditional, absolute, complete love of God. Thus, the statement in verses 4–5:

> *Hear, O Israel: The Lord is our God, the Lord alone. You shall love the Lord your God with all your heart, and with all your soul, and with all your might.*

This would make interesting history except that it is a dream that still affects us today. The land of milk and honey, the promised land with "cities already built and vineyards and olive groves" was a metaphor for that state of union with God, which Jesus later called the Kingdom of Heaven. Fully aware of the traditions of Deuteronomy, Jesus was as unequivocal as Moses. To enter the Kingdom of Heaven was costly and his demands to his disciples (essentially that they had to adhere to the Ten Commandments) required the same absolute devotion as Moses did. Today, it is still just as costly: It remains a demand of complete surrender to the all-defining, all-governing God. The Deuteronomists knew, Jesus knew, and today's church and synagogue know that such perfect obedience is seldom reachable. *But it is the primal goal of faith.*

The command to exclusive loyalty to Yahweh can lead to both despair and pride. Despair may come from always falling short of the goal, possibly leading one to focus excessively on the all-too-readily-available penitential form of worship. Pride can arise from thinking that we are making progress and therefore, are better than others who do not seem so far along the path. Either of these, however, distorts what is intended by God.

The warning issued in this text is just as relevant today in a society as affluent and secure as ours. Ours is an economy of abundance that lives by an ideology of satiation. The seemingly limitless capacity of the consumer economy, supported by a market system that must keep growing, leads to a common, thoughtless assumption that this is the way it should always be.

In our consumer wealth, it is nearly impossible to remember anything important, to remember the kind of discipline required for the creation of the just society, which is God's dream for us. We are satiated to the extent that our lives include nothing of covenantal accountability or the disciplines of covenantal neighborliness.

Chapter 6

More Preamble

Deuteronomy 7
Violence and Vengeance

THERE ARE FOUR PARTS to Deuteronomy 7. It starts off with a gruesome description about what Israel is to do when it meets other nations. This is an example of the violence and vengeance for which the Hebrew scriptures are often condemned. Make no mistake, the orders God has given the Israelites are brutal. By any stretch, the modern reader is sure to find this language deeply offensive and problematic.[1] However, this violence is here. It reflects the thinking of many societies at the time these stories originated and we have to deal with it, so let's look at it.

Deut 7:1–5
Make No Covenant with Other Nations

When the Lord your God brings you into the land that you are about to enter and occupy, and he clears away many nations before you—the Hittites, the Girgashites, the Amorites, the Canaanites, the Perizzites, the Hivites, and the Jebusites, seven nations mightier and more numerous than you— ₂ and when the Lord your God gives them over to you and you defeat them, then you must utterly destroy them. Make no covenant with them and show them no mercy. ₃ Do not intermarry with them, giving your daughters to their sons or

---

1. Remember: This is not a history as we would think. This is a national legend, created, and intended, to make a theological point.

> *taking their daughters for your sons, ₄for that would turn away your children from following me, to serve other gods. Then the anger of the Lord would be kindled against you, and he would destroy you quickly. ₅ But this is how you must deal with them: break down their altars, smash their pillars, hew down their sacred poles, and burn their idols with fire.*

The big fear of Moses (or the Deuteronomists) is that the land of promise is a land filled with seductions, especially the religions of those who already live there. Israel cannot have anything to do with non-Yahwistic gods because those alternative religions will erode the covenant. When the covenant with Yahweh is eroded or compromised, the very survival of the community is placed in jeopardy.[2]

The strategy for dealing with a consumer culture is stated in two very different ways. First, "[Y]ou must utterly destroy." This policy comes from an ancient practice of wholesale destruction of an enemy as an act of theological obedience. This is not as violent as it seems, though, because, by the time it was written, the seven nations named in verse 1 had long since disappeared. They were not a true threat to Israel. (The list of seven nations represented any alien culture with religious temptations for Israel.) Therefore, this text is now to be understood *symbolically, not literally*.

The second proposed strategy (perhaps reflecting later thinking) is not the destruction of the peoples but of their systems of religious symbolization (verse 5). While this is still violent, it is now action committed against religious objects and not against individuals.

Deut 7: 6–11
Yahweh Chooses Israel

> *For you are a people holy to the Lord your God; the Lord your God has chosen you out of all the peoples on earth to be his people, his treasured possession. ₇ It was not because you were more numerous than any other people that the Lord set his heart on you and chose*

---

2. Why the big worry? Today, it is not the end of the world if a Protestant converts to Catholicism or from Christianity to Judaism. But this early time was different because of the huge leap in spiritual consciousness that the Israelites were facing. Think about this: Israel's god has become transcendent and ethical. Yahweh demands complete obedience, radical justice, a radical distribution of resources, and radical morality. How much easier it would be to worship god living in a golden calf, a god that makes no moral or justice demands, and lends itself most willingly to the existing elitist power structure.

> *you—for you were the fewest of all peoples. ₈ It was because the Lord loved you and kept the oath that he swore to your ancestors, that the Lord has brought you out with a mighty hand, and redeemed you from the house of slavery, from the hand of Pharaoh king of Egypt. ₉ Know therefore that the Lord your God is God, the faithful God who maintains covenant loyalty with those who love him and keep his commandments, to a thousand generations, ₁₀ and who repays in their own person those who reject him. He does not delay but repays in their own person those who reject him. ₁₁ Therefore, observe diligently the commandment— the statutes, and the ordinances—that I am commanding you today.*

The text then goes on about why Yahweh chooses Israel.[3] Israel might have thought that it was chosen because Israel is large and impressive, but that is not true. Israel is "fewest." So, the special status is not because of anything Israel has done, it is just that Yahweh "set his heart" on Israel. The verb "set" in Hebrew means a strong emotional attachment that runs beyond any reasonable act. Yahweh made a leap of love in committing to Israel because of Yahweh's ancient oath to the family of Abraham in Genesis.[4]

So, we have a free act by God of commitment to Israel in Genesis (thus creating the "chosen people") but Israel can no longer count on it. According to Deuteronomy, the covenant now works two ways. Yahweh is there to help but only if Israel obeys. And if Israel doesn't obey, its people must reckon with their own self-imposed destruction. The relationship is grounded in free grace, but it has expectations. Everything depends on obedience.[5]

---

3. Keep in mind that today, we would not look at Israel as a people chosen by God. Other peoples may have begun, at the same time or even earlier, to understand God as singular, loving, ethical, and transcendent. We know only that the Israelites were the first to write about it and those writings have been preserved.

4. Genesis 15:1–6 (abridged): "'Do not be afraid, Abram! I am your shield and shall give you a very great reward.' Abram replied, 'what use are your gifts, as I am going on my way childless.' . . . Then Yahweh came to him in reply, '. . . your heir will be the issue of your own body.' Then taking him outside, Yahweh said, 'Look up at the sky and count the stars if you can. Just so will your descendants be,' he told him."

5. There might be a subtle point here that is easy to overlook. Certainly, God is providing free grace, but nowhere does God threaten to remove it. It is implied that the grace is eternal, always available, as Jesus puts it. The consequences of not taking it, therefore, are wholly self-inflicted. This has nothing to do with God taking anything away.

Deuteronomy and Post-Modern Christianity

Deut 7: 12–15
Fertility and Abundance

> *If you heed these ordinances, by diligently observing them, the Lord your God will maintain with you the covenant loyalty that he swore to your ancestors; ₁₃ he will love you, bless you, and multiply you; he will bless the fruit of your womb and the fruit of your ground, your grain and your wine and your oil, the increase of your cattle and the issue of your flock, in the land that he swore to your ancestors to give you. ₁₄ You shall be the most blessed of peoples, with neither sterility nor barrenness among you or your livestock. ₁₅ The Lord will turn away from you every illness; all the dread diseases of Egypt that you experienced, he will not inflict on you, but he will lay them on all who hate you.*

It is interesting to note that the covenant promise here is no longer about having off-spring. It has changed and become material in the form of prosperity for the farming community: animals and fields will produce in abundance. The Israelites don't need to seek agricultural well-being from the gods of the land anymore, for Yahweh is completely capable of being a fertility god. All of the language here has to do with material success, prosperity, abundance, and fertility. The ancestors of Genesis were endlessly vexed about the birth of an heir; now fruitfulness will function on every front. Israel becomes something new, the carrier of the best promises of the creator God. There has never been anything like Israel before in all creation, according to the Israelites. This truly is the first hint of the love of God. It anticipates new creation. The hope for the new land is that it will indeed be the Kingdom of God. But, again, this all relates back to obedience or acceptance of the gift.

One can raise an important point here. Throughout the Hebrew scriptures lies a dichotomy: the contrast between the love of God towards humankind, which is freely given, and the wrath of God, which is a consequence of not loving God in return. This dichotomy is never truly resolved. The love of God certainly evolves throughout the narrative, from the promise of offspring to the promise of a land of milk and honey to a society based on distributive justice. This latter type of society, in effect, refers to an alternative state of consciousness, i.e., being one with God.

But it was still viewed as a conditional love, dependent on obedience to God and subject to dire consequences. Illness, defeat, poverty, drought, and general "bad luck" were still seen as the wrath of God, resulting from not following God's commands. People who did not prosper were thought to be impure. But, a paradigm shift occurred when Jesus came onto the scene. This was one of the main points that Jesus went on about: The love of God was no longer conditional. Bad luck was no longer linked to God nor was it a sign of impurity. God was simply unconditional, non-judgmental love—universal and everlasting—constantly calling us. Needless to say, bad luck or natural calamities did not disappear; they still happened, as they do today. The simple difference was how we viewed such events. They were, and are, no longer God's punishment—just part of life.[6]

Deut 7:16–24
Have No Dread of Other Nations

You shall devour all the peoples that the Lord your God is giving over to you, showing them no pity; you shall not serve their gods, for that would be a snare to you. $_{17}$ If you say to yourself, "These nations are more numerous than I; how can I dispossess them?" $_{18}$ do not be afraid of them. Just remember what the Lord your God did to Pharaoh and to all Egypt, $_{19}$ the great trials that your eyes saw, the signs and wonders, the mighty hand and the outstretched arm by which the Lord your God brought you out. The Lord your God will do the same to all the peoples of whom you are afraid. $_{20}$ Moreover, the Lord your God will send the pestilence against them, until even the survivors and the fugitives are destroyed. $_{21}$ Have no dread of them, for the Lord your God, who is present with you, is a great and awesome God. $_{22}$ The Lord your God will clear away these nations before you little by little; you will not be able to make a quick end of them, otherwise the wild animals would become too numerous for you. $_{23}$ But the Lord your God will give them over to you, and throw them into great panic, until they are destroyed. $_{24}$ He will hand their kings over to you and you shall blot out their name from under heaven; no one will be able to stand against you, until you have destroyed them.

The chapter then reverts back to a harsh dismissal of other peoples, a dismissal that matches the opening lines of verses 1 to 5. These peoples and

---

6. Evil, of course, is a different kettle of fish compared to an earthquake and we might well ask how evil fits into this simple theology. Without any intent whatsoever to deny or diminish the existence or effect of evil in human life, we might view it from the perspective of genetics gone wrong, of bad wiring in the brain. The psychopath, the mass murderer, certainly has what might be called a mental illness. Is that evil?

their religions deeply threaten Israel, because it is so easy to slip out of the obedience that is necessary for Israel to prosper in the land of promise (verse 17).

Deut 7: 25–26
Do Not Covet Icons

The images of their gods you shall burn with fire. Do not covet the silver or the gold that is on them and take it for yourself, because you could be ensnared by it; for it is abhorrent to the Lord your God. $_{26}$ *Do not bring an abhorrent thing into your house, or you will be set apart for destruction like it. You must utterly detest and abhor it, for it is set apart for destruction.*

After the sweeping assurances of verses 18 to 24, Moses issues a final warning about images, thus, returning to the point of verse 5. The repetitiveness of the threats about disobedience may seem boring at first: same old, same old. But let's look at this more deeply. There is an understanding here of what truly drives people. People, then and now, covet the power of the icon. They seek power that permits social control through an appeal to "god" ("God is on our side") and power through wealth: "the silver or the gold."

Some Reflections on Deuteronomy 7

This chapter sees Israel as a radically distinctive community totally committed to Torah obedience. The text acknowledges how hard this is for a community that must live in the real world, one that is full of compelling alternative ways of faith.

Such total commitment to God calls to mind all "communities under discipline": orthodox Jews and Christian sects such as the Amish or peace churches. Those of us on the outside may view such communities as odd. If, however, we think of these "contrast communities" as falling under a *different obedience*, which attempt to be concerned with every aspect of life, we cannot dismiss such disciplines without being aware of how compromised our own mainline forms of faith might be.

We can legitimately ask ourselves if *not* living in a "community under obedience" is, in itself, a compromise of our spiritual goals. Can we and the communities and institutions of our faith truly participate in our society without giving up our ideals, without brushing aside God's dream for us? Is feeling good about attending institutional rituals truly enough? Deuteronomy says that to live with God is exceedingly difficult but the alternative is worse. Jesus said much the same thing.

This chapter of Deuteronomy also reflects the worry of a community in which the children do not join in the faith of their parents. Today, we see our established religious culture in the West in sharp decline. There is smaller and smaller membership and the churches that have survived no longer have significant influence or moral suasion in society at large. The need for major change is obvious but this prospect also makes faith communities deeply anxious. Is God truly telling us to give up our comfortable pew? This chapter may provide a way to think about such anxiety. In our time, as then, what may be happening is not simply a rejection of certain forms of faith, but a rejection of the most basic demands of God.

Some Reflections on Deuteronomy 8

From the perspective of a person of faith in the seventh century BCE, the essential message of Moses was to love God with all of your heart, mind, strength, and soul, and love your neighbor as yourself.

From the perspective of a person of faith in the twenty-first century, the essential message of Moses, the prophets, and Jesus was, and still is: "Love God with all of your heart, mind, strength, and soul" and "Love your neighbor as yourself." But we can rephrase these words today: Become one with God and live in a community of distributive justice.

These words are different but they mean exactly the same thing: Become one with God (an altered state of consciousness) and you will live in the land of milk and honey and in the Kingdom of Heaven. But, if you do not obey these commands, you will live a life of strife, pain, hunger, and death.

Now, the commands to love God and your neighbor truly fall into the same category as saying "Be happy" to someone who is depressed. Life doesn't work that way. Loving God or becoming one with God is not an on-off state. It is a journey, throughout life—an exodus, if you will. Don't forget: we have, perhaps, five thousand years of awareness of right and wrong but as a species, we have maybe fifty million years of survival programming through our DNA. Our conscience tells us to be just and caring in our community but our DNA still drives us to propagate, eat, and survive (in less benign terms, to lust, greed, and have power over others). This is a struggle, one that Deuteronomy so beautifully addresses.

Chapter 8 is brilliant in its eloquent simplicity. It is a concise, plain-spoken summary of everything Moses has said before. It is no less important as a repetition, however. Repetition simply emphasizes the heavy anxiety felt by the Deuteronomists about the loss of identity suffered by the community and the importance of getting it back again. The writers already knew that the people would not necessarily receive the gifts and generosity from Yahweh in gratitude. Gifts given in abundance to the satiated do not result in gratitude and trust but, rather, evoke complacent self-congratulations. Verses 17–18 say it all:

> *Do not say to yourself, "My power and the might of my own hand have gotten me this wealth." $_{18}$ But remember the Lord your God, for it is he who gives you power to get wealth, so that he may confirm his covenant that he swore to your ancestors, as he is doing today.*

In our consumer-satiated world, we think that we gain ownership of things through our own diligence or innate worth, and that we can use our wealth as we see fit, without regard to others. But God's intent is radically different. God's economic plan is much simpler. Creation gives us gifts that allow us to create wealth so that it can be shared equitably by all. A full awareness of God means knowing that all things, all creation, belong only to God. It means wanting to share our wealth with others. All that we have is from creation. We own nothing.

Deut 9, 10, 11
Rules and Regulations Begin

These chapters continue the long preamble to chapter 12, which begins the rules-and-regulations section of Deuteronomy. Moses continues with a long reflection on Israel's past and its sorry relationship with Yahweh to make a point to the then-present generation. (Remember: This document was written in the 500s BCE, during the Babylonian exile, as an imperative to the exiles to regain their unique and radical identity. The writers used the age-old traditional stories of Moses as the basis of their authority.)

More Preamble

Deut 9: 1-2
Hear, O Israel!

Hear, O Israel! You are about to cross the Jordan today, to go in and dispossess nations larger and mightier than you, great cities, fortified to the heavens, ₂ a strong and tall people, the offspring of the Anakim, whom you know. You have heard it said of them, "Who can stand up to the Anakim?"

"Hear, O Israel" is a familiar term, the central claim of Deuteronomy. It means not only to listen up, but also, to submit your entire life to Yahweh in glad dependence and willing obedience. It is the only requirement to enter the land or the Kingdom of God or God-consciousness or to become one with God. This imperative bespeaks trust, confidence, and obedient attentiveness to Yahweh as the sole condition for success, without any reference to wealth, power or arms.

Deut 9: 3-6
The Lord Defeats Wicked Nations

Know then today that the Lord your God is the one who crosses over before you as a devouring fire; he will defeat them and subdue them before you, so that you may dispossess and destroy them quickly, as the Lord has promised you. ₄ When the Lord your God thrusts them out before you, do not say to yourself, "It is because of my righteousness that the Lord has brought me in to occupy this land"; it is rather because of the wickedness of these nations that the Lord is dispossessing them before you. ₅ It is not because of your righteousness or the uprightness of your heart that you are going in to occupy their land; but because of the wickedness of these nations the Lord your God is dispossessing them before you, in order to fulfill the promise that the Lord made an oath to your ancestors, to Abraham, to Isaac, and to Jacob. ₆ Know, then, that the Lord your God is not giving you this good land to occupy because of your righteousness; for you are a stubborn people.

Here, again, lies a reminder that the gifts of God are not some sort of reward for doing good. It is not through our own righteousness that we gain closeness to God. Our righteousness is irrelevant. Charitable donations, feeding the homeless or serving on church committees are not paths to the peace that passes all understanding. It is the exact reverse: good works are a spontaneous, natural outcome of growth in God-consciousness. This is all implicit in Deuteronomy. The reference to the current occupiers of the land that Israel was going to take over is interesting: the Hebrew scriptures are certainly ethnocentric but verses 3 and 4 allude to an awareness by the Israelites that other nations, too, were having their own difficulties with life.

Deut 9: 7–10:11
A Stubborn People

Remember and do not forget how you provoked the Lord your God to wrath in the wilderness; you have been rebellious against the Lord from the day you came out of the land of Egypt until you came to this place. $_8$ Even at Horeb you provoked the Lord to wrath, and the Lord was so angry with you that he was ready to destroy you. $_9$ When I went up the mountain to receive the stone tablets, the tablets of the covenant that the Lord made with you, I remained on the mountain forty days and forty nights; I neither ate bread nor drank water. $_{10}$ And the Lord gave me the two stone tablets written with the finger of God; on them were all the words that the Lord had spoken to you at the mountain out of the fire on the day of the assembly. $_{11}$ At the end of forty days and forty nights the Lord gave me the two stone tablets, the tablets of the covenant. $_{12}$ Then the Lord said to me, "Get up, go down quickly from here, for your people whom you have brought from Egypt have acted corruptly. They have been quick to turn from the way that I commanded them; they have cast an image for themselves." $_{13}$ Furthermore the Lord said to me, "I have seen that this people is indeed a stubborn people. $_{14}$ Let me alone that I may destroy them and blot out their name from under heaven; and I will make of you a nation mightier and more numerous than they." $_{15}$ So I turned and went down from the mountain, while the mountain was ablaze; the two tablets of the covenant were in my two hands. $_{16}$ Then I saw that you had indeed sinned against the Lord your God, by casting for yourselves an image of a calf; you had been quick to turn from the way that the Lord had commanded you. $_{17}$ So I took hold of the two tablets and flung them from my two hands, smashing them before your eyes. $_{18}$ Then I lay prostrate before the Lord as before, forty days and forty nights; I neither ate bread nor drank water, because of all the sin you had committed, provoking the Lord by doing what was evil in his sight. $_{19}$ For I was afraid that the anger that the Lord bore against you was so fierce that he would *destroy you. But the Lord listened to me that time also.* ₂₀ *The Lord was so angry with Aaron that he was ready to destroy him, but I interceded also on behalf of Aaron at that same time.* ₂₁ *Then I took the sinful thing you had made, the calf, and burned it with fire and crushed it, grinding it thoroughly, until it was reduced to dust; and I threw the dust of it into the stream that runs down the mountain.* ₂₂ *At Taberah also, and at Massah, and at Kibroth-hattaavah, you provoked the Lord to wrath.* ₂₃ *And when the Lord sent you from Kadesh-barnea, saying, "Go up and occupy the land that I have given you," you rebelled against the command of the Lord your God, neither trusting him nor obeying him.* ₂₄ *You have been rebellious against the Lord as long as he has known you.* ₂₅ *Throughout the forty days and forty nights that I lay prostrate before the Lord when the Lord intended to destroy you,* ₂₆ *I prayed to the Lord and said, "Lord God, do not destroy the people who are your very own possession, whom you redeemed in your greatness, whom you brought out of Egypt with a mighty hand.* ₂₇ *Remember your servants, Abraham, Isaac, and Jacob; pay no attention to the stubbornness of this people, their wickedness and their sin,* ₂₈ *otherwise the land from which you have brought us might say, 'Because the Lord was not able to bring them into the land that he promised them, and because he hated them, he has brought them out to let them die in the wilderness.'* ₂₉ *For they are the people of your very own possession, whom you brought out by your great power and by your outstretched arm."*

[Deuteronomy ₁₀] At that time the Lord said to me, "Carve out two tablets of stone like the former ones, and come up to me on the mountain, and make an ark of wood. ₂ *I will write on the tablets the words that were on the former tablets, which you smashed, and you shall put them in the ark."* ₃ *So I made an ark of acacia wood, cut two tablets of stone like the former ones, and went up the mountain with the two tablets in my hand.* ₄ *Then he wrote on the tablets the same words as before, the ten commandments that the Lord had spoken to you on the mountain out of the fire on the day of the assembly; and the Lord gave them to me.* ₅ *So I turned and came down from the mountain, and put the tablets in the ark that I had made; and there they are, as the Lord commanded me.* ₆ *(The Israelites journeyed from Beeroth-bene-jaakan to Moserah. There Aaron died, and there he was buried; his son Eleazar succeeded him as priest.* ₇ *From there they journeyed to Gudgodah, and from Gudgodah to Jotbathah, a land with flowing streams.* ₈ *At that time the Lord set apart the tribe of Levi to carry the ark of the covenant of the Lord, to stand before the Lord to minister to him, and to bless in his name, to this day.*

> *₉ Therefore Levi has no allotment or inheritance with his kindred; the Lord is his inheritance, as the Lord your God promised him.) ₁₀ I stayed on the mountain forty days and forty nights, as I had done the first time. And once again the Lord listened to me. The Lord was unwilling to destroy you. ₁₁ The Lord said to me, "Get up, go on your journey at the head of the people, that they may go in and occupy the land that I swore to their ancestors to give them."*

This is a recap of the traditional narrative. It tells of a thousand, maybe even two thousand, years in which humankind had already been struggling with right and wrong, at least in what grew to be the Judeo-Christian-Islamic culture. Some translations of Deuteronomy use the term "stiff-necked" for stubborn. This idiom comes from an agrarian background. Oxen can be stubborn. When they do not want to be harnessed, they make their neck stiff, which prevents proper positioning of the yoke around their neck.

Verses 10: 6–9 are believed to be an editorial insert. The journey and brief reference to Aaron, Eleazar, and Levi may reflect an old and deep tension among different priestly communities. Ultimately, the tradition holds that the tribe of Levi became the successor to Moses. The Levites were never to receive land; rather, they were to be the priestly house. Without a vested interest in land, they could be considered honest and trustworthy.

Deut 10: 12–22

> *So now, O Israel, what does the Lord your God require of you? Only to fear the Lord your God, to walk in all his ways, to love him, to serve the Lord your God with all your heart and with all your soul, ₁₃ and to keep the commandments of the Lord your God and his decrees that I am commanding you today, for your own well-being. ₁₄ Although heaven and the heaven of heavens belong to the Lord your God, the earth with all that is in it, ₁₅ yet the Lord set his heart in love on your ancestors alone and chose you, their descendants after them, out of all the peoples, as it is today. ₁₆ Circumcise, then, the foreskin of your heart, and do not be stubborn any longer. ₁₇ For the Lord your God is God of gods and Lord of lords, the great God, mighty and awesome, who is not partial and takes no bribe, ₁₈ who executes justice for the orphan and the widow, and who loves the strangers, providing them food and clothing. ₁₉ You shall also love the stranger, for you were strangers in the land of Egypt. ₂₀ You shall fear the Lord your God; him alone you shall worship; to him you shall hold fast, and by his name you shall swear. ₂₁ He is your praise;*

> he is your God, who has done for you these great and awesome things that your own eyes have seen. ₂₂ Your ancestors went down to Egypt seventy persons; and now the Lord your God has made you as numerous as the stars in heaven.

This unit is one of the loveliest and most powerful summations of covenant theology offered in the book of Deuteronomy. It makes a bid for Israel's most serious and willing obedience to Yahweh, just because of who Yahweh is and what Yahweh has done. It is clear that the appeal here is not to occupy the land but to embrace the Torah.

The unit begins with a rhetorical question concerning Yahweh's intention for Israel. Verses 12–13 give answer to the question: *fear* [7] Yahweh, *walk* in Yahweh's ways (commands), *love* Yahweh, and *serve* Yahweh fully. These four verbs refer to a complete commitment to Yahweh without reserve, a readiness to be fully identified with, and by, Yahweh and to enact that identity through an intentional and distinctive way in the world. Yahweh requires Israel to devote all of its life, nothing less.

Verse 16 commands the nation to "circumcise . . . the heart," and "do not be stubborn." This must have referred to the long-standing practice of circumcision as a way to signify membership in the covenant with Yahweh.[8] Here, the ritual practice of circumcision becomes a metaphor for intense loyalty to Yahweh.

Note that the High God of verse 17 is also a God very involved in the affairs of the earth. *This point is key.* Their God is a God who cannot be bribed by the wealthy and powerful but who attends to the needs and wishes of orphans and strangers, and who cares about justice. Israel is the recipient of Yahweh's *transformative justice*, which becomes a staple of covenant

---

7. As noted earlier, the term "fear" does not mean "Be afraid." Its archaic use here refers to a sense of awe, reverence, and mystery, far beyond our capacity to understand.

8. Circumcision is far older than recorded history. Certainly, it is far older than the biblical account of Abraham in (Genesis 17). It seems to have originated in eastern Africa, long before this time. Many theories have been advanced to explain its origin. One is that circumcision began as a way to purify individuals and society by reducing sexuality and sexual pleasure. Another relates it to long-ago snake worship in Egypt, since snakes shed their skin. The Jews adopted circumcision as a religious ritual in prehistoric times but tradition holds that Moses and his sons were not circumcised. (Exodus 4:25). Although Moses apparently prohibited circumcision during the forty years in the wilderness (Joshua 5:5), Joshua reinstituted circumcision after the death of Moses (Joshua 5:2–10).

ethics. God's will is simply the full caring for the vulnerable in society.[9] God always pushes us outside safe religion to the work of human community. And, regardless of the Israelites' view that they were the chosen people, their ethics (their radical identity) had to extend even to the stranger. Israel is not permitted to become a homogeneous, ethnic community turned in on itself, but must, as a part of its most basic responsibility, extend its transformative justice beyond itself to those who do not belong.

This was God's dream five thousand years ago in the prophets, in Jesus, and it remains God's dream today. Yet our modern mainline religions (Jewish and Christian) have become so domesticated, so much a part of the consumer-military system, that their distinctiveness is almost gone. Mainstream religious institutions appear to pay only lip service to radical identity, content to tinker only at the edges of our modern societies, which are primarily hierarchical and rooted in retributive justice.[10]

So, the imperatives of Deuteronomy 10:12–22 are still there. They are an invitation, once again, to become Yahweh's special people. Such a step offers any community a radical newness but cannot be just a casual hobby. This is an invitation that means business. A recovery of identity as God's people would have made the unnoticed little community of Israel formidable in the world. Today, it doesn't take much to imagine how any unnoticed little community, which lived by God's covenant, would also become formidable, would become the conscience of our society. There is no real alternative.

Some Reflections on Deuteronomy 11

This chapter concludes the introduction to the statutes and ordinances that began in chapter 5. The themes of this chapter are, by now, familiar. The argument here is not difficult to follow. But because the writers believed it necessary to repeat these themes over and over, this suggests that the Babylonian exiles did not put the covenant into practice. Deuteronomy is a mature statement of how faith is to be understood and practiced. It makes

---

9. When we experience the love that we call God, we have no choice but to become concerned about the plight of the poor, the sick, the addicted, and the abandoned.

10. This is not to say that Israel ever achieved the ideal society. Israel was no more successful in developing a community free of retributive justice and hierarchical societies than we are today. Remember: the Deuteronomists had two agendas: to describe God's ideal and lay down guidelines for community as it worked towards the ideal.

no claim that it reflects true history. Rather, its intent is to call the exiles to a more radical, single-minded practice: exclusive loyalty to God and attentiveness to the neighbor.

In our modern time and place, we do not face the identity crisis that once challenged the exiled Jews. Nevertheless, a great many of us continue to seek true meaning in life. We struggle hard, only to find that a high standard of living in itself seems to provide nothing but more grief. It is no wonder. The growth of production creates wealth, and the growth of wealth becomes centralized, concentrated more and more in the hands of the few. Wealth for the sake of wealth becomes an insatiable addiction. It is easy to see that such acquisitive power, with its privatization and the loss of a sense of the public good, threatens the fabric of the larger human community. Such unlimited individualism means, sooner or later, the loss of a viable humanness and a growth of brutality, anxiety, loneliness, and despair.

The concern for teaching the faith and marking it visibly (verses 18 to 21) is to produce a Torah community immune to the seductions of other types of security. That way, these seductions hold no allure for the young. Indeed, that is the educational burden of every self-aware community of passionate conviction. Its work is to hold its young and protect them from seduction by the ideology of *autonomy*, enacted through money-sex-power, the great triad of self-possession.

With the conclusion of the rhetoric of chapters 5 to 11, the speech of Moses shifts to the details, the "statutes and ordinances" of how to live in the land. This begins the second agenda of Deuteronomy mentioned in the introduction. The material that follows is diverse and variegated, and probably has a complex history of origin, development, and transmission. In the final form of the text, it is offered, despite its diversity, as a single, unified teaching, all of which bears the urgency of Mosaic imperative. Israel must heed all of it!

Chapter 7

Right Living: The Statutes and Ordinances

CHAPTER 3 INTRODUCES THE notion that the Deuteronomists had two agendas, the first talking about allowing God to be the sole focus of Israel's life and the second telling how to live while awaiting the first. We can consider this section as the beginning of the second agenda. The purpose of this section of Deuteronomy is to bring every aspect of the public life of Israel under the rule of God. Yahweh demands that Israel develop social practices that are radically different yet compatible with the character and will of Yahweh. Yahweh is to be visible to others through the public policies and daily actions of Israel.

A long scholarly debate concerns the shape and arrangement of this extended list of statutes and ordinances. The collection is almost completely random; each commandment must be taken on its own terms. On the other hand, there might be some organizing principle behind them, but nothing is certain. We take them as they come.

The initial thrust of these statutes and ordinances is that Israel must worship God correctly because the focus of Israel's worship will determine the quality of its life.

Deut 12: 1–7
Avoid Seductive Threats

These are the statutes and ordinances that you must diligently observe in the land that the Lord, the God of your ancestors, has given you to occupy all the days that you live on the earth. ₂ You must demolish completely all the places where the nations whom you are about to dispossess served their gods, on the mountain heights, on

Right Living: The Statutes and Ordinances

> *the hills, and under every leafy tree. ₃ Break down their altars, smash their pillars, burn their sacred poles with fire, and hew down the idols of their gods, and thus blot out their name from their places. ₄ You shall not worship the Lord your God in such ways. ₅ But you shall seek the place that the Lord your God will choose out of all your tribes as his habitation to put his name there. You shall go there, ₆ bringing there your burnt offerings and your sacrifices, your tithes and your donations, your votive gifts, your freewill offerings, and the firstlings of your herds and flocks. ₇ And you shall eat there in the presence of the Lord your God, you and your households together, rejoicing in all the undertakings in which the Lord your God has blessed you.*

We get into viciousness right from the start, but the issue is important enough to warrant such language.[1] Israel must resist the worship practices of the culture that it will already find in the land of promise. These alternative practices are a seductive threat to Israel. If they are embraced even a little, they will take Israel out of Yahweh's covenant. Indeed, the danger is so great that Israel must destroy all anti-covenantal images. The writer probably has no interest in the particulars of pagan cult objects and perhaps, no specific knowledge of them either. They are treated, *en masse*, as a threat to Israel. The banned items are to be replaced by a catalogue of sacrifices in verse 6. Following these rules will culminate in joy. This joy, moreover, is quite material: food, milk and honey, and fertile land. Joyous eating, by itself, becomes right worship. Life is to be a festival in which Israel exhibits, and enjoys, the blessings of God.

Again, note: the Kingdom of God is not described here as some mystical state of spiritual awareness. It is concrete, a land of milk and honey, focusing on an abundance of produce for all. Later, prophets and Jesus start changing the focus from food and drink to living in a state of full awareness of God. Nothing is changed, even today. We can express this as follows:

> *Obedience = Land of Milk and Honey =*
> *Kingdom of God = God-consciousness*

---

1. We saw this viciousness towards worship practices of other gods earlier in Deut 7; it is so important that it needs repeating. But remember: It isn't as bad as it seems at first glance because the language is rhetorical. Nevertheless, the motivation driving this rhetoric is extremely serious. Yahweh is laying out a very difficult path, one quite impossible to truly follow. Hence, a less demanding lifestyle becomes very tempting.

We can interpret this to mean that people who grow deeply into communion with God will always have plenty to eat.[2]

Deut 12: 13–16
Make One Central Place for Animal Slaughter

> *Take care that you do not offer your burnt offerings at any place you happen to see. $_{14}$ But only at the place that the Lord will choose in one of your tribes—there you shall offer your burnt offerings and there you shall do everything I command you. $_{15}$ Yet whenever you desire you may slaughter and eat meat within any of your towns, according to the blessing that the Lord your God has given you; the unclean and the clean may eat of it, as they would of gazelle or deer. $_{16}$ The blood, however, you must not eat; you shall pour it out on the ground like water.*

This marked major changes to daily life. Previously, altars were spread throughout the land, and animals slaughtered on the altars were completely consumed by flame. But now it was decreed that there be only one central place for the sacrifice. The slaughtered animal was no longer lost, except for its blood, which was to be poured onto the ground. The rest of the animal was to be cooked, rather than burned to a crisp, then shared equitably by all members of the community, i.e., God gives back to the community the very thing that the community offered up. This recognizes that all of life is a gift from God. God does not need to consume what is needed by God's people.

Almost as an aside, verse 15 refers to clean and unclean meat. The origins of "clean" and "unclean" animals are lost to prehistory, but several large religions, besides Judaism, maintain these concepts. The idea that some animals are dangerous or disgusting is present in almost all known human cultures. This could be because people in ancient times had not realized how to preserve and prepare some foods. For instance, pork not prepared or stored properly can cause illness, as can some seafood. Pigs can also transmit flu to humans from birds. Labeling the animal as unclean and

---

2. This raises an intriguing question. Today, the world population is growing rapidly and wealthy nations continue to hoard food while most of humanity goes hungry. When the whole world achieves God-consciousness and hence, everyone has enough to eat, does this mean that everyone will naturally eat less? Does it mean that there is already enough food in the world and we will just start sharing equitably? Or does it mean the earth will somehow become more productive?

forbidden prevented the consumption and handling of these potentially dangerous foods.³

Deut 12:17–19
Correct Tithing Brings Blessings

> Nor may you eat within your towns the tithe of your grain, your wine, and your oil, the firstlings of your herds and your flocks, any of your votive gifts that you vow, your freewill offerings, or your donations; ₁₈ these you shall eat in the presence of the Lord your God at the place that the Lord your God will choose, you together with your son and your daughter, your male and female slaves, and the Levites resident in your towns, rejoicing in the presence of the Lord your God in all your undertakings. ₁₉ Take care that you do not neglect the Levite as long as you live in your land.

The second-rule change concerns tithing. Again, it was to be done centrally. This list acknowledges Yahweh's ownership of all, for the tithe is like the tenant's rent paid to the landowner. As with the sacrifice, the Israelites receive back the tithe given as an acknowledgment of Yahweh's sovereignty over the land. God, as the "owner" of the land, is not greedy or parsimonious, and wants nothing for self. Thus, Israel may enjoy one-hundred percent of the produce of Yahweh's blessing in Yahweh's land.

Deut 12:20–28
Eat Meat Whenever You Desire

> When the Lord your God enlarges your territory, as he has promised you, and you say, "I am going to eat some meat," because you wish to eat meat, you may eat meat whenever you have the desire. ₂₁ If the place where the Lord your God will choose to put his name is too far from you, and you slaughter as I have commanded you any of your herd or flock that the Lord has given you, then you may eat within your towns whenever you desire. ₂₂ Indeed, just as gazelle or deer is eaten, so you may eat it; the unclean and the clean alike may eat it.

---

3. Or, as an alternative theory, perhaps clean and unclean is about clarifying that humans do not own everything. The more arbitrary the unclean food, the better. God is not negotiable or explainable, thus some foods are purely arbitrarily forbidden so that at every meal we remember the reality of God.

> ₂₃ Only be sure that you do not eat the blood; for the blood is the life, and you shall not eat the life with the meat. ₂₄ Do not eat it; you shall pour it out on the ground like water. ₂₅ Do not eat it, so that all may go well with you and your children after you, because you do what is right in the sight of the Lord. ₂₆ But the sacred donations that are due from you, and your votive gifts, you shall bring to the place that the Lord will choose. ₂₇ You shall present your burnt offerings, both the meat and the blood, on the altar of the Lord your God; the blood of your other sacrifices shall be poured out beside the altar of the Lord your God, but the meat you may eat. ₂₈ Be careful to obey all these words that I command you today, so that it may go well with you and with your children after you forever, because you will be doing what is good and right in the sight of the Lord your God.

This section reflects changes to the previous section concerning centralization. Verses 13 to 19 are likely older and for a small farming community. Small communities do not have a problem with centralization but larger ones will. Thus, verses 20 to 27 might be reflecting, later, a bigger community. Some Israelites live far from "the place" (early regional planning, if you will). These verses seem to suggest that Israelites are permitted to eat and enjoy at home if they live far from the main place of worship. God does not intend to make worship a hardship for people who live on the outskirts.

Deut 12: 29–32
Diligently Observe Right Worship

> When the Lord your God has cut off before you the nations whom you are about to enter to dispossess them, when you have dispossessed them and live in their land, ₃₀ take care that you are not snared into imitating them, after they have been destroyed before you: do not inquire concerning their gods, saying, "How did these nations worship their gods? I also want to do the same." ₃₁ You must not do the same for the Lord your God, because every abhorrent thing that the Lord hates they have done for their gods. They would even burn their sons and their daughters in the fire to their gods. ₃₂ You must diligently observe everything that I command you; do not add to it or take anything from it.

The final unit of this chapter is peculiarly intense, and may have been added after verse 28 to emphasize right worship. This statement is a warning, once again, about the power of reverting to the old way of living, for it

Right Living: The Statutes and Ordinances

will continue to seduce even after it has been destroyed. The word "imitation" calls to mind the tendency to return to a monarchy like the reign of Solomon. Indeed, for Deuteronomy, Solomon was a terrible king. He is the great case study in compromise and entrapment, which leads to exile (1 Kgs 11:5–7). The term "abomination" comes easily to the lips of the Deuteronomists when contemplating Solomon.

Child sacrifice is brought up at the end of this chapter. It would appear that the practice of child sacrifice was still around. The much earlier story of Abraham and his son indicated that Israelite society was wrestling with the issue at that time. Now, many centuries later, a firm stand exists against this practice.

Some Reflections on Deuteronomy 12

This chapter of Deuteronomy emphasizes the dangers of humans thinking that they are autonomous from God. A secular society asserts that humans are the source of culture and religion, that we are our own law. It rejects the notion of absolute good or truth. At best, it rises to the concept of the greater good of society. However, those who seriously explore their own spiritual natures will generally acknowledge, in some form, that an absolute good or absolute truth exists. It exists, in and of itself, without boundaries, and transcends all of humanity and the universe. Deuteronomy knew this and cautions against the destructive illusion that we are the center of our own life.

No doubt, such self-indulgence is a huge temptation in contemporary Christian worship. Worship today is often reduced to therapeutic self-help and self-enhancement. It is offered in simplistic stories and sweetness without any notion of covenantal requirement or rigor. Such a romantic-therapeutic distortion of worship is powerfully attractive, precisely because it requires almost nothing from us. It is clear that most North American churches and temples buy into market capitalism mixed with a celebration of power. Of course, this buy-in is couched in the language of piety and altruistic goodwill, assuming that this ideology, in no way, is contrary to the gospel. We maintain class consciousness, self-enrichment, power over others, and retributive justice. Do we truly believe that this is not contrary to a God who has no form and who will not be reduced to any domesticated pattern?

Deuteronomy and Post-Modern Christianity

Deuteronomy offers a sharp contrast to this buy-in. It is to the God of Deuteronomy that Israel, as written in this chapter, brings its offerings and responds in joyous, inclusive sharing.

At the Jordan River, Moses reluctantly lays down for Israel an urgent, costly,[4] and non-negotiable option of either-or: Israel must either choose Yahweh or not. Israel must choose to be the people of Yahweh or not. And in these choices, Israel will choose to live well in the land of promise or not.

---

4. As before, "costly" does not imply money. It refers to the cost of giving up, completely, a comfortable, safe, familiar lifestyle for an unknown future of total obedience to God. Again, this is not a matter of will or of trying. Instead, it is a naturally occurring outcome of gaining complete God-consciousness. Although it sounds harsh and comes at a high cost, total obedience to God truly becomes effortless, pure joy and love.

Chapter 8

Do's and Don'ts

NOW WE GET DOWN to the nitty-gritty of what it means to live day-to-day, according to God's law. The do's and don'ts are simple and very clear. Following them, however, is another story.

Deut 14: 1–21
Here's What's Holy and What's Not

You are children of the Lord your God. You must not lacerate yourselves or shave your forelocks for the dead. $_2$ For you are a people holy to the Lord your God; it is you the Lord has chosen out of all the peoples on earth to be his people, his treasured possession. $_3$ You shall not eat any abhorrent thing. $_4$ These are the animals you may eat: the ox, the sheep, the goat, $_5$ the deer, the gazelle, the roebuck, the wild goat, the ibex, the antelope, and the mountain-sheep. $_6$ Any animal that divides the hoof and has the hoof cleft in two, and chews the cud, among the animals, you may eat. $_7$ Yet of those that chew the cud or have the hoof cleft you shall not eat these: the camel, the hare, and the rock badger, because they chew the cud but do not divide the hoof; they are unclean for you. $_8$ And the pig, because it divides the hoof but does not chew the cud, is unclean for you. You shall not eat their meat, and you shall not touch their carcasses. $_9$ Of all that live in water you may eat these: whatever has fins and scales you may eat. $_{10}$ And whatever does not have fins and scales you shall not eat; it is unclean for you. $_{11}$ You may eat any clean birds. $_{12}$ But these are the ones that you shall not eat: the eagle, the vulture, the osprey, $_{13}$ the buzzard, the kite, of any kind; $_{14}$ every raven of any kind; $_{15}$ the ostrich, the nighthawk, the sea gull, the hawk, of any kind; $_{16}$ the little owl and the great owl, the water hen $_{17}$ and the desert owl, the

> carrion vulture and the cormorant, $_{18}$ the stork, the heron, of any kind; the hoopoe and the bat. $_{19}$ And all winged insects are unclean for you; they shall not be eaten. $_{20}$ You may eat any clean winged creature. $_{21}$ You shall not eat anything that dies of itself; you may give it to aliens residing in your towns for them to eat, or you may sell it to a foreigner. For you are a people holy to the Lord your God. You shall not boil a kid in its mother's milk.

To summarize the preceding passage, this chapter starts off with these directives:

- You must not lacerate yourselves.
- You must not shave your forelocks for the dead.
- You must not eat any abhorrent thing. (A comprehensive list is given.)
- You must not eat anything that dies of itself.
- You must not boil a kid in its mother's milk.[1]

There seems to be no logic to this list. The text gives no explanation of the significance of these practices, nor why they are linked to living in accordance with Yahweh's way. We are not aware of any prehistory for the list, no evidence of it developing over time. However, it is hard to imagine a group of writers making it up themselves. Scholarship has been noticeably unsuccessful in interpreting these prohibitions.

Regardless, since each of these injunctions begins with a command to be holy, they do become the dividing line between what is holy and what is not, between clean and unclean. The rules separate sacred and profane, even in ordinary, day-to-day living, or especially, in day-to-day living. Rules like these keep God front and center. God is not a once-a-week, special occasion.

These rules, however, were causing considerable problems by Jesus' time. Let's look at this for a moment. Earlier, this book stated that the Ten Commandments were possibly the naturally occurring behaviors of people who had reached a state of close communion with God. There is something universal and eternal about them. But the prohibition against eating winged insects does not have an eternal ring to it in the same way. The list, as it stood, certainly would provide a unique identity to the nation and, as

---

1. It would be extremely difficult and cruel to boil a kid in its mother's milk. There is no history of this ever being a real practice. It is possibly a mistranslation of the forbidden practice of cooking a kid in milk of any kind. This might have been borrowed from some other community in prehistory.

just mentioned, would act as a constant reminder about honoring Yahweh. But after the Babylonian exile ended (it lasted only a century or so), the need for a unique identity was no longer an urgent matter of life and death for the culture. As well, those who truly lived their lives honoring Yahweh would never, even from the start, think of clean and unclean food in the same way that a literal fundamentalist would. Hence, Jesus, as a Jewish reformer, campaigned against those who practiced the letter rather than the spirit of the law. He did not stand against tradition *per se*, when it supported spiritual development. He stood against tradition that was exclusionary and judgmental, which categorized *people* as clean or unclean.

Jesus reinterpreted the conventional rules of holiness, changing their direction almost completely. We no longer see particular items emphasized as a measure of holiness and there is a much-less-tangible focus on discerning God's will. This certainly reflects a more sophisticated understanding of God. Not eating pig is one thing but, obviously, discerning God's will is a whole different ballgame. This is not to say that traditions and uniqueness do not have their own value; again, it is a matter of degree.

The Beginning of Social Legislation

Now comes a series of rules that define the radical and alternative covenant society. They concern tithing (paying rent), forgiveness of debt, and the release of slaves. The tithing reflects that Yahweh is the landlord and owns the land (people only "rent" it). The remission of debt and release of slaves further remove any sense of ownership or wealth grab by individuals. Not many loopholes here.

Deut 14: 22–29
How to Tithe and Distribute Funds

> Set apart a tithe of all the yield of your seed that is brought in yearly from the field. $_{23}$ In the presence of the Lord your God, in the place that he will choose as a dwelling for his name, you shall eat the tithe of your grain, your wine, and your oil, as well as the firstlings of your herd and flock, so that you may learn to fear the Lord your God always. $_{24}$ But if, when the Lord your God has blessed you, the distance is so great that you are unable to transport it, because the place where the Lord your God will choose to set his name is too far

> *away from you, ₂₅ then you may turn it into money. With the money secure in hand, go to the place that the Lord your God will choose; ₂₆ spend the money for whatever you wish—oxen, sheep, wine, strong drink, or whatever you desire. And you shall eat there in the presence of the Lord your God, you and your household rejoicing together. ₂₇ As for the Levites resident in your towns, do not neglect them, because they have no allotment or inheritance with you. ₂₈ Every third year you shall bring out the full tithe of your produce for that year, and store it within your towns; ₂₉ the Levites, because they have no allotment or inheritance with you, as well as the resident aliens, the orphans, and the widows in your towns, may come and eat their fill so that the Lord your God may bless you in all the work that you undertake.*

The statute on the tithe concerns the public management and distribution of funds under the covenant. The tithe is a tax paid to the owner of the land who has a claim on its produce. When the tithe is understood as a tax, to whom is it owed? Such a tax was likely paid to imperial overlords (see 1 Sam 8:15–17). In the view of Deuteronomy, however, neither the king nor any alien imperial power could claim a tithe because none of them is the rightful owner of the land. Yahweh is.

The primary statute concerning the tithe is simple and direct. In a farm economy, a yearly harvest determines how much is "owed" to Yahweh, who owns the land. The tithe must be brought to that place where Yahweh chooses as an acknowledgment of the unequal relationship of owner and tenant. This tithe, however, is unlike any other tax or payment made to the owner, because this owner (Yahweh) does not want or need the tithe that Israel offers (see Ps 50:9–13).[2]

Instead, the tithe brought to "the place" is promptly given back to the people of Israel, who are to eat and enjoy the offering that it has brought. Again, note that this tithe is to be shared equally by all. The offering goes to Yahweh, who gives it right back to the people. Why bother? Yahweh does not want the produce, but insists on the gesture that acknowledges Yahweh's generous sovereignty.

In what must be a subsequent development of the statute, these verses assume that as the territory of Israel expands, the transport of produce

---

2. To quote the psalm: *"I will not accept a bull from your house, or goats from your fold. I know all the birds of the air, and all that moves in the field is mine. If I were hungry, I would not tell you, for the world and all that is in it is mine. Do I eat the flesh of bulls, or drink the blood of goats? Offer to God a sacrifice of thanksgiving, and pay your vows."*

Do's and Don'ts

becomes inconvenient. To accommodate such a geographical reality, produce can be converted into cash that can then, at the place, be converted back into produce to be enjoyed by the whole community.

Yahweh's community is comprehensive. It allows for a priestly caste. Verse 27 provides for the inclusion of Levites, the priestly teaching community that has no land, and therefore, no produce for the tithe, in the celebration. The Levites are the carriers of the Mosaic tradition. Their mention here ensures that the tithe will be kept within the framework of the covenantal vision that Deuteronomy lays out.

Deut 15: 1
No Debt Bond to Exceed Seven Years

Every seventh year you shall grant a remission of debts.

We now turn to the issue of debt. That ancient economy managed it in a manner not too different from today's ways. Those who accrued debt had to work it off as bond servants; consequently, the length of service correlated with the size of the debt. Those who owed more had to work longer to pay off the debt. Those with huge debts had to work them off seemingly forever. The teaching here breaks the endless term of debt and work by limiting the bond to seven years, no matter how great the debt. This is radical, for it completely subverts the usual practices of loans, credits, interest, and debt management by which any common economy functions.

Deut 15:2–6
Debtors and Creditors are Equal

And this is the manner of the remission: every creditor shall remit the claim that is held against a neighbor, not exacting it of a neighbor who is a member of the community, because the Lord's remission has been proclaimed. $_3$ Of a foreigner you may exact it, but you must remit your claim on whatever any member of your community owes you. $_4$ There will, however, be no one in need among you, because the Lord is sure to bless you in the land that the Lord your God is giving you as a possession to occupy, $_5$ if only you will obey the Lord your God by diligently observing this entire commandment that I command you today. $_6$ When the Lord your God has blessed you, as he

> *promised you, you will lend to many nations, but you will not borrow; you will rule over many nations, but they will not rule over you.*

Verse 1, in all of its bluntness, now receives explanation. This regulation is designed to strengthen the Israelite community. The creditors and debtors are both called "neighbor" and "brother or sister," implying a relationship that transcends economic reality: they are equal. In this community, economics does not define people; rather, what defines them is a common memory of the Exodus, a common blessing in the land, and a common allegiance to the God of Exodus and land.

Then comes a provision that is against short-term economic interest. The urgent tone suggests that nobody except Yahweh owns anything. Although the injunction to release debts seriously undermines normal economics, it will really work: a land overflowing with Yahweh's abundance allows Israel to be generous to a neighbor. Greed and exploitation are inappropriate in a land of such prosperity.

Deut 15: 7–11
Give to Needy Neighbors

> *If there is among you anyone in need, a member of your community in any of your towns within the land that the Lord your God is giving you, do not be hard-hearted or tight-fisted toward your needy neighbor. 8 You should rather open your hand, willingly lending enough to meet the need, whatever it may be. 9 Be careful that you do not entertain a mean thought, thinking, "The seventh year, the year of remission, is near," and therefore view your needy neighbor with hostility and give nothing; your neighbor might cry to the Lord against you, and you would incur guilt. 10 Give liberally and be ungrudging when you do so, for on this account the Lord your God will bless you in all your work and in all that you undertake. 11 Since there will never cease to be some in need on the earth, I therefore command you, "Open your hand to the poor and needy neighbor in your land."*

"Anyone in need" tells those with land to take care of the landless and vulnerable. The statute insists that those with land *have that land precisely to feed all*. That is their responsibility. It's that simple.

Verses 7 to 8 warn against being "hard-hearted" and "tight-fisted." This happy translation refers to the rich who live in reflexive fear, resistance, resentment, and indifference. These are the kinds of responses that the poor tend to evoke in the well-off: fear of having to share, of losing control.

Verse 9 warns against a form of "logical" thinking. Because Yahweh is so committed to neighborly justice in the covenant community, the uncared-for and needy may appeal to Yahweh against the unresponsive neighbor who has resources. Social transactions in Israel are never between two parties, but always take place in the presence of Yahweh; this third party will powerfully sustain the entitlements of the poor against the rich.

The warning is matched by an assurance (verses 10–11). Attentiveness to the poor through debt cancellation will evoke more blessing from Yahweh. Generosity to the neighbor will result in greater generosity from Yahweh. Generosity evokes generosity.

Deut 15: 12–17
Wealth Belongs to God

> *If a member of your community, whether a Hebrew man or a Hebrew woman, is sold to you and works for you six years, in the seventh year you shall set that person free. $_{13}$ And when you send a male slave out from you a free person, you shall not send him out empty-handed. $_{14}$ Provide liberally out of your flock, your threshing floor, and your wine press, thus giving to him some of the bounty with which the Lord your God has blessed you. $_{15}$ Remember that you were a slave in the land of Egypt, and the Lord your God redeemed you; for this reason I lay this command upon you today. $_{16}$ But if he says to you, "I will not go out from you," because he loves you and your household, since he is well off with you, $_{17}$ then you shall take an awl and thrust it through his earlobe into the door, and he shall be your slave forever. You shall do the same with regard to your female slave.*

The act of cancelling debt is not enough. Debt cancellation by itself would send the poor person back on the street without any resources. Such a person would have no chance of survival and would soon be back in debt. This loophole is promptly closed with verses 13 to 14. Cancelling debt is followed by an order to also finance the poor person (from the blessings of flock, field, and vineyard received from Yahweh) well enough to start over. Again and again, these statutes remind those with wealth that it is not *their* wealth—it belongs to God.

Obviously, this is not a popular command from God. It might be the hardest of all provisions because many people express the sentiment: "We worked hard for our comfortable life." So, the supreme appeal for compliance with this regulation has to be the memory of the Exodus. Earlier verses have already suggested that prosperity can lead to amnesia. Amnesia invites people to think that the current dramatic distinction between haves and have-nots, rich and poor has always been this way and is probably rightly deserved. Not so. The memory of Exodus makes clear that what the rich have is not an entitlement; it is simply a gift to be used to help others. Creditors and debtors have a lot more in common than they have differences.

Of course, some debt slaves may renounce freedom and remain bonded. They may do this out of a sense of well-being in a good relationship with their "owners." Allowance is made for this.

Deut 15: 18
To Free Former Debt Slaves is No Hardship

Do not consider it a hardship when you send them out from you free persons, because for six years they have given you services worth the wages of hired laborers; and the Lord your God will bless you in all that you do.

The final appeal in verse 18 indicates, yet again, that there must have been a lot of opposition to this radical economic provision. The resistance is for the obvious reason that the statute takes money out of people's pocket. The God of the covenant requires definite limits on money-making.

Some Comments on Debt Cancellation

Debt cancellation is the centerpiece of a radically alternative vision of economics that defines the covenant community. The economy is very much secondary to the community and must be made to serve and enhance that community, not rule it. There is to be no permanent underclass. We can't overstate how radical and crucial this provision is. It insists on nothing less than an economy in which creditors and debtors are bound together. They are equal and have a common destiny rooted in Yahweh.

Do's and Don'ts

This vision of a neighborly economy, moreover, knows that debt management defines the society. What a society does about debt, how lenders manage debt, and whether borrowers are respected or reduced to long-term poverty determines whether there will be shared, common peace and prosperity or prosperity only for the lenders. A society filled with restless debtors keeps the entire community in turmoil, under threat, and lacking in peace.

It is clear, moreover, that the economic vision of a neighborly society stands in complete opposition to the more conventional economic practices in every society, including today's ideology of the free market and its privatization. The ideology of privatization is an economic claim that private prosperity is legitimate, without any obligation to the neighborhood or to the maintenance of the social fabric.

Deut 15: 19–23

> *Every firstling male born of your herd and flock you shall consecrate to the Lord your God; you shall not do work with your firstling ox nor shear the firstling of your flock. $_{20}$ You shall eat it, you together with your household, in the presence of the Lord your God year by year at the place that the Lord will choose. $_{21}$ But if it has any defect—any serious defect, such as lameness or blindness—you shall not sacrifice it to the Lord your God; $_{22}$ within your towns you may eat it, the unclean and the clean alike, as you would a gazelle or deer. $_{23}$ Its blood, however, you must not eat; you shall pour it out on the ground like water.*

This section bridges economics and worship. The provision for sacrifice of a firstling, the first male lamb or calf, belongs under the "right worship of Yahweh." The sacrifice of the first animal is a common enough routine, an acknowledgement that it is a gift from Yahweh to be returned to Yahweh in gratitude. But it has a distinct Israelite twist. First, Yahweh does not need the sacrifice brought to Yahweh. It is returned for the joyous consumption of the worshiping community. Second, the animal is not to be "worked." This is the same Hebrew term for the word "slave." An offering to Yahweh has to be from the sphere of freedom that allows no bondage (work).

Verses 21 to 23 plug a loophole. A firstborn lamb or calf may be less than perfect, of course. Such an animal would be an inappropriate sacrifice. The ban on defective animals says that Yahweh must have the best that Israel has. Yahweh is not a God to be addressed with leftovers. Yahweh comes first.

Today, it is especially easy to gloss over this routine statute without realizing its real cost. Consider the command "all your heart, all your mind, all your substance" (as in 6:5). Yahweh must come first. Yahweh demands this. But as we become autonomous, seemingly independent of others, this demand by God tends to lose its force.

1. Instead of *"all your heart"* in our emotionally draining, anxiety-driven society, God receives the leftovers of commitment. We often arrive at Yahweh emotionally exhausted with nothing left to give.

2. Instead of *"all your mind,"* faith increasingly falls victim to a dumbing-down process. Hence, claims of faith, in relation to life's hard issues, do not receive the best critical thought. Allowing faith to become a mindless, self-preoccupied enterprise is like bringing a defective animal for sacrifice.

3. Instead of *"all your substance"* in a self-indulgent, overspent, over-mortgaged society, we most often donate to God and charities only the portion of our income that we can afford. After budgeting for everything else that we want to spend our money on, these are mere leftovers.

A spent emotional life, intellectual laziness and indifference, and a penny-pinching, self-absorbed economic life are the same as bringing defective animals to Yahweh's place. They demean Yahweh and compromise Yahweh's vision of what counts. Those who live in this way imagine life on their own terms, yielding nothing, grateful for nothing, generous about nothing. The routine sacrifice of unblemished firstlings is a regular gesture of discipline that serves to keep Israel's priorities straight.

Chapter 9

Take Time to Be Holy

So far, times of worship in Israel have shown no overall pattern. Several festivals already existed but did not appear in an orderly way. Rather, they arose ad hoc out of a variety of historical memories and agricultural festivals already common in the region. Moreover, the liturgical calendar of Israel was not stable and constant, but shaped and reshaped over time by a variety of circumstances and needs. The Deuteronomists here offer a complete calendar, more or less, to bring a regularized pattern to the annual festival cycle.

Deut 16: 1–8
Religious Observance Keeps the Story Alive

Observe the month of Abib by keeping the Passover for the Lord your God, for in the month of Abib the Lord your God brought you out of Egypt by night. ₂ You shall offer the Passover sacrifice for the Lord your God, from the flock and the herd, at the place that the Lord will choose as a dwelling for his name. ₃ You must not eat with it anything leavened. For seven days you shall eat unleavened bread with it—the bread of affliction—because you came out of the land of Egypt in great haste, so that all the days of your life you may remember the day of your departure from the land of Egypt. ₄ No leaven shall be seen with you in all your territory for seven days; and none of the meat of what you slaughter on the evening of the first day shall remain until morning. ₅ You are not permitted to offer the Passover sacrifice within any of your towns that the Lord your God is giving you. ₆ But at the place that the Lord your God will choose as a dwelling for his name, only there shall you offer the Passover sacrifice, in the evening at sunset, the time of day when you departed

> *from Egypt. ₇ You shall cook it and eat it at the place that the Lord your God will choose; the next morning you may go back to your tents. ₈ For six days you shall continue to eat unleavened bread, and on the seventh day there shall be a solemn assembly for the Lord your God, when you shall do no work.*

While the Passover emerged as a defining festival in Judaism, the references to it in the Hebrew scriptures are sparse (see Exod 12–13; 2 Kgs 23:21—23). The festival here is kept focused upon the exclusive agenda of Deuteronomy. The unleavened bread, described in Exod 12–13, is bread that was eaten "in haste," without waiting long enough for the yeast to rise, in order to flee the Pharaoh. So, eating unrisen bread at night is to replicate the moment of escape from Egypt and the freedom that resulted on that night.

The primary purpose of the festivals is truly for the Israelites to remember their story and to pass it on from generation to generation.[1]

Deut 16: 9–12
Keep the Festival of Weeks for the Lord

> *You shall count seven weeks; begin to count the seven weeks from the time the sickle is first put to the standing grain. ₁₀ Then you shall keep the festival of weeks for the Lord your God, contributing a freewill offering in proportion to the blessing that you have received from the Lord your God. ₁₁ Rejoice before the Lord your God—you and your sons and your daughters, your male and female slaves, the Levites resident in your towns, as well as the strangers, the orphans, and the widows who are among you—at the place that the Lord your God will choose as a dwelling for his name. ₁₂ Remember that you were a slave in Egypt, and diligently observe these statutes.*

The "festival of weeks" is the second great festival. The word "weeks" here comes from the number seven. The festival calendar is a complex rhythm of sevens, reflecting the Sabbath principle. Perhaps the rhythm of the agricultural seasons lies behind that.[2] In Exodus 23:16, the same celebration is

---

1. The depth of tradition that Deuteronomy was trying to establish is perhaps analogous to that of Christmas. Although concerned only with secular issues of family and gift-giving, not with spiritual issues, Christmas is certainly a deep part of North American tradition, which is passed on generation to generation.

2. The seven-day week probably derived from ancient Babylon religions. Its exact origin is unknown.

termed a "harvest festival"; there is no doubt that it is related to the harvest of crops. In an agricultural society, this is a make-or-break occasion when the entire income of the year is produced.

Because of the productivity of the land, the festival focuses on blessing. This most broadly connects the event to creation and the goodness of the Creator. The creator God has guaranteed fruitfulness, which makes a bountiful harvest possible.

Deut 16: 13–15
Booths Festival: Embrace History and Gratitude

You shall keep the festival of booths for seven days, when you have gathered in the produce from your threshing floor and your wine press. ₁₄ Rejoice during your festival, you and your sons and your daughters, your male and female slaves, as well as the Levites, the strangers, the orphans, and the widows resident in your towns. ₁₅ Seven days you shall keep the festival for the Lord your God at the place that the Lord will choose; for the Lord your God will bless you in all your produce and in all your undertakings, and you shall surely celebrate.

The third festival in the calendar is Booths (Tabernacles). Booths are temporary shelters. Most likely, this festival was originally agricultural, perhaps with booths built to protect crops from the hot sun. Booths could also remind the Israelites of the story of the temporary shelters used during their time in the wilderness. Thus, a festival readily holds together the combination of land blessing and historical memory, in the service of generating a great public exhibit of gratitude.

Deut 16: 16–17
All Males to Appear at Three Great Festivals

Three times a year all your males shall appear before the Lord your God at the place that he will choose: at the festival of unleavened bread, at the festival of weeks, and at the festival of booths. They shall not appear before the Lord empty-handed; ₁₇ all shall give as they are able, according to the blessing of the Lord your God that he has given you.

This summary names the three great festivals and specifies three duties.

First, the festivals concern all the males in the community. One may wonder why only males are mentioned, as the festivals elsewhere in the Bible were more inclusive. This likely reflects the conflict between the patriarchy of the past and the attempt to become more inclusive.

Second is another reminder that participation in the festivals is an act of gratitude, that offerings are part of them. The offering signifies both Yahweh's sovereignty (ownership of the land) and gratitude. "Empty-handed" celebrants can't come because being "empty-handed" signifies a reluctance to acknowledge Yahweh and an unwillingness to give public expression to gratitude.

Third, all the males "shall appear." There is no doubt that this is non-negotiable. Membership in the covenant community requires public participation. The festival is a visible public act. What it most requires is showing up, seen to be engaged in Yahwistic activity, seen by the young of the community, by non-Israelite neighbors. Responsible adults visibly declare a rejection of other loyalties and sources of well-being. The festival is a declaration of a decision about life-and-death blessing-and-curse.

These festivals in Israel represent the act of an alternative community, one that stands apart from the brick quotas of the pharaoh (forced labor imposed by alien rulers), Canaanite seductions, and the difficult choices and ambiguous realities of daily life. Here, Israel enters a zone where the awesome generosity of the earth receives full play. During the festivals, Israelites again remember that their freedom is not their own work, but a gift gladly given by Yahweh. Israel also acknowledges the generous productivity of the earth so that Yahweh gives grain, wine oil, herds, and flocks in abundance without any productive engineering by Israel.

In our current time and place, we might wonder if a festival can have such power and attractiveness. We combine complacency, self-indulgence, and individual autonomy as a year-round festival at consumer outlets like Costco and Walmart. Deuteronomy prompts the question: Today, can we have liturgical festivals as credible and compelling as consumer festivals that are better funded?[3] Gratitude is a condition that our dominant culture resists. Yet, that very gratitude becomes the entry point to the festival,

---

3. The modern calendar of the church revolves around its three great festivals of Christmas, Easter, and Pentecost. Pondering the festivals of ancient Israel may lead to reflection on how these Christian festivals, too, are moments outside time.

wherein the new community of God becomes reality. Small wonder that it is important to show up.

Chapter 10

Justice: True, Honest Justice

AT THIS POINT, THE rules and regulations in Deuteronomy turn from personal to civil order. As has been true for virtually all societies, including today's, the concept of justice remains relative. Generally, the rich and powerful are the ones who make up the rules, which are intended to maintain the position of the rich and powerful. But Yahweh's dream has a different end in mind: absolute justice, especially for those who are not rich and powerful. Therefore, the general theme of this next section of Deuteronomy is the covenantal deployment of public power. This is not a series of platitudes, however: it is a serious theory of power. Four "offices" or functions of power and leadership— judge(s), king, priest(s), and prophet— model the distribution of public powers in ways to avoid corruption or distortion; they describe how power can work in a covenantal community. Each function is important in itself. Together, they show a covenantal vision of public power.

Deut 16: 18–22
Justice Must be Blind and Ethical

> *You shall appoint judges and officials throughout your tribes, in all your towns that the Lord your God is giving you, and they shall render just decisions for the people. $_{19}$ You must not distort justice; you must not show partiality; and you must not accept bribes, for a bribe blinds the eyes of the wise and subverts the cause of those who are in the right. $_{20}$ Justice, and only justice, you shall pursue, so that you may live and occupy the land that the Lord your God is giving you. $_{21}$ You shall not plant any tree as a sacred pole beside the altar*

that you make for the Lord your God; ₂₂ nor shall you set up a stone pillar—things that the Lord your God hates.

A commitment to justice and its administration are basic to covenantal society. These verses provide a sketch of what such a judicial system might look like. The expectations that judges and officials be responsible and trustworthy are clear. Judges are told the following:

- Do not distort justice;
- Do not show partiality;
- Do not accept bribes.

The concern is that justice must be genuinely disinterested and not influenced by the special pressure that the rich and powerful are able to exercise, for the latter group, characteristically, are the ones who can offer bribes and purchase partiality. Secondly, this regulation explicitly mentions the poor, who must be protected by the court because they likely have no other social guarantee or advocate. To put it another way: God is looking over the shoulder of the judge.

Deut 17: 2–7
Severe Penalties Protect a Community

You must not sacrifice to the Lord your God an ox or a sheep that has a defect, anything seriously wrong; for that is abhorrent to the Lord your God. ₂ If there is found among you, in one of your towns that the Lord your God is giving you, a man or woman who does what is evil in the sight of the Lord your God, and transgresses his covenant ₃ by going to serve other gods and worshiping them—whether the sun or the moon or any of the host of heaven, which I have forbidden—₄ and if it is reported to you or you hear of it, and you make a thorough inquiry, and the charge is proved true that such an abhorrent thing has occurred in Israel, ₅ then you shall bring out to your gates that man or that woman who has committed this crime and you shall stone the man or woman to death. ₆ On the evidence of two or three witnesses the death sentence shall be executed; a person must not be put to death on the evidence of only one witness. ₇ The hands of the witnesses shall be the first raised against the person to execute the death penalty, and afterward the hands of all the people. So you shall purge the evil from your midst.

The second section of this law works out procedures for reliable testimony. The Scripture here is brutal but the case cited about serving other gods is crucial, intended to serve as a model for all cases. There is no distinction between violations against Yahweh and civic violations against a neighbor; they are one and the same. So, the important point here is not to base communal discipline on rumor or hearsay. A careful judicial investigation is required to determine the facts of the case. Other testimony must support the accuser. It is assumed that the accused is innocent until proven guilty. Mind you, being proven guilty brings the death penalty. The book of Deuteronomy is committed to a rule of law, even if it is a severe one. Execution for offences might seem barbaric to us now but, remember: this is from twenty-five hundred years ago. Protection of the community from distortion was a life-and-death issue. An interesting twist is added: the one who makes the accusation must initiate the execution, supported by the participation of the entire community.

Deut 17: 8–13
God's Vision is the Ultimate Law

> *If a judicial decision is too difficult for you to make between one kind of bloodshed and another, one kind of legal right and another, or one kind of assault and another—any such matters of dispute in your towns—then you shall immediately go up to the place that the Lord your God will choose, ₉ where you shall consult with the Levitical priests and the judge who is in office in those days; they shall announce to you the decision in the case. ₁₀ Carry out exactly the decision that they announce to you from the place that the Lord will choose, diligently observing everything they instruct you. ₁₁ You must carry out fully the law that they interpret for you or the ruling that they announce to you; do not turn aside from the decision that they announce to you, either to the right or to the left. ₁₂ As for anyone who presumes to disobey the priest appointed to minister there to the Lord your God, or the judge, that person shall die. So you shall purge the evil from Israel. ₁₃ All the people will hear and be afraid, and will not act presumptuously again.*

The third part of a court system provides for a central court that can take over truly difficult cases from local village courts. The example of difficult cases in verse 8 is open-ended, not limited to homicide and assault. What counts the most here is that the hard cases will be heard at "the place" where

Justice: True, Honest Justice

Yahweh is intensely present and where Yahweh's public officials are most informed about Yahwistic justice. More specifically, along with judges and officials, now the Levite priests are involved in judging, which means a move toward the covenantal will of God.

The amount of space given to ensure compliance is surprising. Compliance to law is a make-or-break issue in the community, and no departure from exact compliance will be tolerated. This is the bottom line: God's vision is the ultimate law. The punishment of those who do not comply with this is death, to discourage others' resistance or indifference to the court in times to come.

It is clear that biblical faith cares about public power. It specifically intends that public power shall be in the interest of God's justice. This is important, particularly in today's environment of both church and society, in which faith is often reduced to personal, privatized matters of a romantic, therapeutic kind. True faith can only be enacted in public. The Bible is about the reordering of public life under the rule of God. It insists that public power is the place where the deepest claims of faith operate.

The community, then and now, sees a clear law and order that does not tolerate deviation. This is not as simple as it sounds, however. First, it is clear that the law and order assumed here does not defend the status quo or a bland system of sanctions. Rather, this is justice that comes from the God of widows and orphans. The commitment to law and order has a theological dimension—it is the God of covenant, of social solidarity, who evokes judicial practice. At the same time, this justice has an important economic dimension. The theory of justice in Deuteronomy contains the seeds of distributive justice, which protects the disadvantaged. There is no exploitation or dishonesty, or anything that is not of benefit for the more disadvantaged party.

Second, in the times of Deuteronomy, like today, punishment was the sentence for breaking the law. But in the last hundred years or so, we have thrown in a component of rehabilitation with punishment. It is no stretch of the imagination to see from Deuteronomy that God's social vision today (Love your neighbor as yourself) would do away with the punishment bit altogether. We aren't quite there yet as a society, though; our penal system still reflects our social uncertainty by providing the worst of both.

Finally, in this form of justice, it is the work of the central court to interpret or convert social vision to particular cases. The practice of justice is not a series of fixed codes and automatic sanctions; rather, it is a practice of covenantal interpretation that serves the larger vision of society. It is absolute justice in every sense. This text might be an invitation to the church today to take up afresh the deep commitments of affirmative social justice. Unlike a system in which the powerful make the laws, which are slanted to maintain their power, the text tells us to recover a central commitment to God's justice in our practice of justice.

Deut 17: 14–15
Seek a King Chosen by God

When you have come into the land that the Lord your God is giving you, and have taken possession of it and settled in it, and you say, "I will set a king over me, like all the nations that are around me," $_{15}$ you may indeed set over you a king whom the Lord your God will choose. One of your own community you may set as king over you; you are not permitted to put a foreigner over you, who is not of your own community.

The second public official is the king. This is the only real statute on kingship in the Torah. This is strange considering the strong presence of the monarchy in the life of ancient Israel. This monarchy was a source of much dispute in that community because many exploitative kingships had reigned prior to, and all around, the Israel of ancient times. Israel also faced internal tensions around village autonomy versus centralized power.

Deut 17: 16–17
Horses, Wives, and Riches: Maintain Distributive Power

Even so, he must not acquire many horses for himself, or return the people to Egypt in order to acquire more horses, since the Lord has said to you, "You must never return that way again." $_{17}$ And he must not acquire many wives for himself, or else his heart will turn away; also silver and gold he must not acquire in great quantity for himself.

There are three very insightful "do nots" here:

1. Do not multiply horses. Since they are a symbol and measure of power, the reference is to the development of a strong military force. The writers know that a strong military power is much less likely to

be responsible to the covenant. A strong military power will think it does not need God or will claim that God is on its side. The "return to Egypt" warns against the reduction of Israel, once again, to slavery. A king with an insatiable military budget taxes his own people into economic dependence. Historically, this provision reflects Solomon's horse trading, whereby Israel became an arms dealer, a practice surely contrary to Yahweh's desire. Either way, the acquisition of horses signifies the undoing of covenantal Israel;

2. Do not multiply wives. This is probably not a comment on monogamy or adultery. More likely, it is a reflection on Solomon, who cemented political alliances through marriages so that his marriages were political arrangements (he accumulated seven hundred foreign wives plus three hundred concubines.[1] The danger of accumulating royal wives is that the alliances and political commitments they come with are simply another way to grab more power; and

3. Do not multiply silver and gold. Silver and gold in large quantities signal a state committed to opulence and self-aggrandizement. This achievement is possible only by the transfer of tax moneys in exploitative ways. There is no doubt, yet again, that Solomon is indeed the model here, for his Jerusalem establishment became a showcase for conspicuous consumption. Solomon's regime had become completely self-serving, predictably to the neglect of the kind, neighborly concerns that lie at the heart of the covenant. The writers seem to make Solomon the worst-case scenario for what happens when concentrated power disregards the covenant and its commitment to distributive power and justice.

Deut 17: 18–20
A Wise King Follows God's Law

When he has taken the throne of his kingdom, he shall have a copy of this law written for him in the presence of the Levitical priests. $_{19}$ It shall remain with him and he shall read in it all the days of his life, so that he may learn to fear the Lord his God, diligently observing all the words of this law and these statutes, $_{20}$ neither exalting himself above other members of the community nor turning aside from the

---

1. 1 Kings 11

> *commandment, either to the right or to the left, so that he and his descendants may reign long over his kingdom in Israel.*

Moses offers an alternative to self-serving power and greed. If having a king is necessary, then his role is to spend primary energy on the study of the Torah, instructed and tutored by the Levites.[2] What will protect kingship from greed and self-destruction is precisely the Torah of Deuteronomy. Deuteronomy makes the institution of monarchy subordinate to the Torah, responsive to the regulations of Moses.[3] The writers did not think that just reading a scroll would change public matters. Rather, leaders must be totally immersed in God's vision. The text is an invitation for a community of faith to rethink public power and the relationship of the governed to the governors. Deuteronomy insists that the powerful in both state and church are subject to a will and purpose other than their own.

Three aspects of this issue merit further attention. First, it is clear in the Christian scriptures that Jesus was exceedingly selfless in his life and teachings. In Matthew 6:25–33, Jesus advises his disciples against anxiety. Even in the circles of the most powerful, then and now, it is anxiety for more—more power, wealth, security, pleasure, beauty, and influence—that propels arrogant power. It is no accident that Jesus cites Solomon as the typically anxious one who, in all his power and wealth, turned out to be second-rate.

Second, this provision is a warning to the community of faith. In our society, free-market ideologies of self-advancement deeply affect the church and temple. Those who become leaders do not worry about horses and wives as much as about silver and gold. It is evident, moreover, that in a rich society, local congregations are sorely tempted towards extravagant buildings and programs by spending Torah funds that might be otherwise deployed.

Third, it is perhaps public leadership today and not church and temple leadership that might be most in the purview of this statute. When western European and North American governments increasingly become the

---

2. The provision is that the king shall have a "copy of this Torah." In Greek, the term "copy" means a second version. From this verse, the book of Deuteronomy takes its popular name as a second version of the Torah of Sinai. Thus, the book of Deuteronomy is not the document of Sinai but a second, derivative, more expansive vision from the God of Sinai.

3. The durability of monarchy depends on compliance with the Torah. The subsequent disregard of the Torah by several kings leads to land loss and deportation. This is the story told in 1 Kings and 2 Kings.

monopoly of the wealthy, and legislation pays special attention to corporate management, which cares only about profit, then a Torah-based social vision that recognizes every person's entitlements is difficult to keep in focus. The cynicism of self-serving power is deathly to the spirit of those who are powerful. They become slaves—comfortable slaves, no doubt—but slaves nevertheless. Plain and simple, Moses asserts that leadership devoted to the accumulation of wealth, power, influence, and prestige, in the public or private management domain, is a way to social disintegration. The Torah keeps the managers of power fixed on the social fabric and on the neighbor who has no horses, no silver, no gold, and perhaps only one wife or husband.

To put this in simpler terms: Our leaders need to be very wise in the ways of God. They should also be reluctant to have power. Why should we elect people who *want* to be elected so that they can become the rule-makers?

Deut 18: 1–8
Celebrate a Priest Without Property

The Levitical priests, the whole tribe of Levi, shall have no allotment or inheritance within Israel. They may eat the sacrifices that are the Lord's portion $_2$ but they shall have no inheritance among the other members of the community; the Lord is their inheritance, as he promised them. $_3$ This shall be the priest's due from the people, from those offering a sacrifice, whether an ox or a sheep: they shall give to the priest the shoulder, the two jowls, and the stomach. $_4$ The first fruits of your grain, your wine, and your oil, as well as the first of the fleece of your sheep, you shall give him. $_5$ For the Lord your God has chosen Levi out of all your tribes, to stand and minister in the name of the Lord, him and his sons for all time. $_6$ If a Levite leaves any of your towns, from wherever he has been residing in Israel, and comes to the place that the Lord will choose (and he may come whenever he wishes), $_7$ then he may minister in the name of the Lord his God, like all his fellow-Levites who stand to minister there before the Lord. $_8$ They shall have equal portions to eat, even though they have income from the sale of family possessions.

Traditionally, the Levites were the one Israelite tribe designated to be priests for all the other tribes. Because they were priests, they did not inherit any land and, so, were exempted from the distractions of commerce. In spite of lacking direct connection to the land, the Levites long ago became an enduring ruling force in Israel. The third office in this "constitution," therefore, is the Levitical priest. This text reinforces that Israel must have Levitical priests and must be prepared to pay for this. These verses make two provisions. First, rather than Yahweh's goods or properties, Yahweh himself is the inheritance of the tribe of Levi. The gift of Yahweh himself is regarded as a great gift, perhaps greater than a parcel of land. The priests are the symbol that prevents social life from being flattened into one of commodity. The priesthood handles the core symbols of faith, and the nurture and practice of such a presence in the community is deeply important.

But, second, this leaves a problem: one cannot turn Yahweh into food. Levi may "have" Yahweh but that is not a visible means of support. For that reason, verse 2 is matched in verse 1. The offerings made to Yahweh become the means of maintenance for these priests.

A couple more points arise. Since the priesthood lies outside the economic processes, this results in a life of freedom. These priests enjoy freedom from normal, social entitlements, a freedom that has the prospect of genuine spiritual creativity. Especially today, this is no small matter. In our modern society, the priest is vulnerable to the standards and politics of a greed-driven economy. But this model, in which Levitical priests have no stake in the economy and depend on Israelites who bring offerings, is to be celebrated. It offers a model of living by the generosity of others.

Though the text concerns priesthood, it is worthwhile to ponder more generally the phrase, "Yahweh is my portion." The Levitical priests are mandated to an extreme form of covenantal living that concerns all members of the community. The acceptance of Yahweh as "portion" to the exclusion of all other portions is a remarkable check upon the attraction of consumer goods. Extreme consumerism—the mad pursuit of a portion—is both the cause and consequence of a lack of intimacy with Yahweh, who is a true portion for those in covenant. Yahweh as portion, in contrast to all other portions, suggests a radical either/or, a choice fully between portion as *communion* and portion as *commodity*.

Deut 18: 9–14
Israel Must Choose Its Future

When you come into the land that the Lord your God is giving you, you must not learn to imitate the abhorrent practices of those

Justice: True, Honest Justice

> nations. ₁₀ No one shall be found among you who makes a son or daughter pass through fire, or who practices divination, or is a soothsayer, or an augur, or a sorcerer, ₁₁ or one who casts spells, or who consults ghosts or spirits, or who seeks oracles from the dead. ₁₂ For whoever does these things is abhorrent to the Lord; it is because of such abhorrent practices that the Lord your God is driving them out before you. ₁₃ You must remain completely loyal to the Lord your God. ₁₄ Although these nations that you are about to dispossess do give heed to soothsayers and diviners, as for you, the Lord your God does not permit you to do so.

Ways of predicting the future were highly common and attractive in the days of Deuteronomy. Knowing about the future was important for a society, for it related to both planning and hope. In particular, it reflected the anxiety of a farming economy that always lay at the mercy of the elements. The writers, in their wisdom however, realized that predicting the future was nothing but smoke and mirrors and it exploited others. Such practices were contrary to covenant because trying to control the future implied that the future is fixed and settled; in other words, people were subject to a fate already decreed. But under God, the future was not a settled fate but an open destiny. It was up to Israel to choose that future.

This cannot be overemphasized: Divination denied the freedom of responsibility for both the people and Yahweh. These abominations were totally contrary to God's dream, producing a society of apathy and manipulation in which human choice, freedom, and responsibility were rendered null and void.

The positive alternative to these rejected practices appears in verse 13: "You shall be completely loyal." This represented a total commitment without reservation. So, the only way to ensure the future was through these practices:

- offering sacrifices to Yahweh and support the priests assumed to be deeply immersed in God;
- canceling debts; and
- loving your neighbor, including the stranger.

Jesus' teaching reflects the same message in Matt 5:48: *"Be perfect, therefore, as your heavenly Father is perfect."*

This translation is not completely correct because the term "perfect" suggests a kind of moral perfection. That is not what Jesus was saying. In both Deut 18:13 and Matt 5:48, the summons is of another kind: namely, unreserved loyalty or obedience to God. Israel then, and we today, are called to fully depend on Yahweh, without seeking to manage the future.

Deut 18: 15–22
A Prophet Ensures Covenant Loyalty

> *The Lord your God will raise up for you a prophet like me from among your own people; you shall heed such a prophet. $_{16}$ This is what you requested of the Lord your God at Horeb on the day of the assembly when you said: "If I hear the voice of the Lord my God any more, or ever again see this great fire, I will die." $_{17}$ Then the Lord replied to me: "They are right in what they have said. $_{18}$ I will raise up for them a prophet like you from among their own people; I will put my words in the mouth of the prophet, who shall speak to them everything that I command. $_{19}$ Anyone who does not heed the words that the prophet shall speak in my name, I myself will hold accountable. $_{20}$ But any prophet who speaks in the name of other gods, or who presumes to speak in my name a word that I have not commanded the prophet to speak—that prophet shall die." $_{21}$ You may say to yourself, "How can we recognize a word that the Lord has not spoken?" $_{22}$ If a prophet speaks in the name of the Lord but the thing does not take place or prove true, it is a word that the Lord has not spoken. The prophet has spoken it presumptuously; do not be frightened by it.*

The fourth "office" in the covenant-community-to-come is a prophet. Today, we think of a prophet as one who predicts the future, but this is not the proper understanding.[4] Placing the prophet alongside judges, priests, and a king says that the prophet is as crucial to a covenant society as the other more common-sense positions. The prophet is the one who will ensure that Israel remains completely loyal to covenant. The function of the prophet is to remind people constantly about God's dream for us.[5] Of course, there are

---

4. This misunderstanding may stem from the Christian practice of interpreting parts of the Hebrew scriptures as foretelling the coming of Jesus. This was never the intent of the prophets. Further, there is little historical evidence that any but a few Israelites anticipated the arrival of a god-like messiah. The term "messiah" referred to a fully human king who would be anointed by a priest. Only then would he be deemed to have been sent by Yahweh.

5. In other words, the prophet is both observer and color commentator, if you will. The prophet knows what should be and comments on what is truly happening. Often, the prophet's comments were said to have been generated in a dream or vision.

real prophets and false ones. How to tell the difference? How do we truly discern God's will from those who claim that God's will gives them power over our money? There is no simple answer. The answer must truly come from God. This is the rub: the prophet must discern God's will, but so must we in order to know real truth.

Further, we know that the community is not autonomous. The ideology of autonomy, expressed today as a free market and the practice of privatization, tends to assert that those with power, wealth, and knowledge, whether individuals, corporations or nation states, are free to do whatever they want. Deuteronomy completely dismisses that notion. It also dismisses social stratification and the myth of a natural law that keeps people in their place.

To summarize this section of Deuteronomy, the easiest temptations, *autonomy* (thinking that our individual actions have no consequences for others) and *fatedness* (thinking that the status quo is the natural order of things), basically say that there is no God with the authority to command and to transform. In the face of two such powerful assumptions, as powerful today as back then, the prophet bears witness to the reality that human life is under a covenant with God (or a covenant with absolute truth and goodness, for those who do not like the term God). After the verdict of the *judges*, after the rule of the *king*, and after the sacrifices and instructions of the *priests*, Israel with the *prophet* comes to the verb "listen." In listening comes human responsibility for a just present. In listening comes human possibility for the future. The prophet permits Israel to hear, and to do.

19: 1–13
Break the Vicious Cycle of Violence

When the Lord your God has cut off the nations whose land the Lord your God is giving you, and you have dispossessed them and settled in their towns and in their houses, $_2$ you shall set apart three cities in the land that the Lord your God is giving you to possess. $_3$ You shall calculate the distances and divide into three regions the land that the Lord your God gives you as a possession, so that any homicide can flee to one of them. $_4$ Now this is the case of a homicide who might flee there and live, that is, someone who has killed another person unintentionally when the two had not been at enmity before: $_5$ Suppose someone goes into the forest with another to cut wood, and when

> *one of them swings the ax to cut down a tree, the head slips from the handle and strikes the other person who then dies; the killer may flee to one of these cities and live. ₆ But if the distance is too great, the avenger of blood in hot anger might pursue and overtake and put the killer to death, although a death sentence was not deserved, since the two had not been at enmity before. ₇ Therefore I command you: You shall set apart three cities. ₈ If the Lord your God enlarges your territory, as he swore to your ancestors—and he will give you all the land that he promised your ancestors to give you, ₉ provided you diligently observe this entire commandment that I command you today, by loving the Lord your God and walking always in his ways—then you shall add three more cities to these three, ₁₀ so that the blood of an innocent person may not be shed in the land that the Lord your God is giving you as an inheritance, thereby bringing bloodguilt upon you. ₁₁ But if someone at enmity with another lies in wait and attacks and takes the life of that person, and flees into one of these cities, ₁₂ then the elders of the killer's city shall send to have the culprit taken from there and handed over to the avenger of blood to be put to death. ₁₃ Show no pity; you shall purge the guilt of innocent blood from Israel, so that it may go well with you.*

Here begins a series of texts in seemingly random order. First, we are concerned with the danger of murder and its resulting cycle of murder. The mention of cities set apart as places of sanctuary is an attempt to curb the vicious cycles of violence in the community.

Homicide happens. It may be intentional or unintentional. In an agrarian tribal society, families have long memories of grievance and honor. In the heat of this honor, the "avenger of blood" does not stop to ask if the initial death is accidental and, indeed, does not care. Blood requires blood. The next-of-kin of the slain person must simply kill the murderer in revenge. The second family must then retaliate. On it goes in an unending cycle of violence. To stop this, Deuteronomy establishes cities of refuge. An accused murderer may be pursued and needs to able to reach protection promptly. The initial notion of asylum is for any homicide, that is, all murderers. While guilt and innocence will be decided later, the idea at the outset is unconditional safety to any comer, without any initial questioning. This reduces the danger of mindless retaliation.

Then comes the judgment. For example, the first case concerns an accidental death. The statute specifies that if there was no bad blood between the two parties before the death, it is assumed that it was an accident and the accused is innocent. This averts the very real danger of a bloodbath.

On the other hand, the accused is judged guilty if there has been malice aforethought, a pre-existing condition of hate. In that case, the elders who manage the whole process willingly let the killer be killed by blood revenge. The judges only judge; it is up to the aggrieved to seek vengeance. This is a nice twist. When the condition of guilt is satisfied, the elders get out of the way and the old processes of family vengeance kick in. The execution of the guilty by the victim's kin ends the power of blood guilt by answering it. End of revenge. It's pretty crude, but certainly a large step beyond endless cycles of blood guilt.

This law has a very narrow agenda. It is not soft on crime—quite the contrary. Within its own context, the law vigorously affirms capital punishment, albeit the rough procedure of a tribal society.

Some Thoughts on Violence, Asylum, and God's Presence

1. The issue of vengeance is huge in any society, because uncontrolled vengeance makes life unlivable. When a blood avenger kills an innocent neighbor in retaliation for an earlier murder, honor requires that the avenger should then be killed, and on and on and on. Therefore, every society that intends to be stable must face the problem of vengeance and devise ways to limit it. The Deuteronomists dealt with it brilliantly. It would be nice to think that the modern world has evolved beyond such practices. Yet, the sectarian killings in northern Ireland, which are inexplicable to outsiders, or the ethnic cleansing in the Balkans or in central Africa, or the endless retaliation in the Middle East and Afghanistan indicate that these places have no public institutions that can be trusted. Thus, any system that stands between the *instinct for revenge* and *protection of the public* is an important one.

   Today, we still need institutions that can restrain violence because the hunger for vengeance is clearly still with us, even among people of faith. In spite of romantic notions of forgiveness, we have to recognize a deep necessity for retribution; it may be channeled and restrained, but still not denied. Those who advocate for the death penalty and for tougher laws and jail sentences are up front, at least, about the deep instincts embedded in all of us.[6] We have to give this instinct

---

6. Our DNA retains the primitive instincts to survive, to propagate, and to eat, which guaranteed our evolution from primal protoplasm. These instincts are stored in our brain stem along with basic activities such as digestion, heartbeat, etc. The survival instinct

the respect it deserves before we can truly start to deal with it. We haven't done that yet. We cannot decide if our prison system is one of punishment or rehabilitation. We lock up prisoners, but give them counseling and programs and training.

2. The matter of asylum concerns other social issues as well. Namely, these are situations in which the powerful, to gain even more power, pursue the powerless, who never have enough leverage to protect themselves, let alone retaliate. Consider, for example, defenseless refugees and political fugitives who seek sanctuary from aggressive regimes. Or "illegal" immigrant workers hunted down by government agencies. Or the most desperate drug addicts and sex-trade workers in our cities who are barred from services that are there to help. The offering of sanctuary, or as current rhetoric says, "open and affirming spaces," is of critical importance if society is to honor humanness beyond the satiation of rage, hatred, and vengeance. "Cities of refuge" is an ancient notion but is no less pertinent in a society that has not evolved beyond elemental violence in the name of honor and justice.

3. Where is God in this issue? If you are reading this book, you are most likely not one of the marginalized or helpless. It should be very clear where God is. Deuteronomy states, in no uncertain terms, that we are to love our neighbor as ourselves. "But," we say, "how can I love my mugger or rapist or those who defraud me?" Generally, we cannot.[7] Human life is life at risk. No matter how much we pray, God does not provide a "safe place." Yes, it is Yahweh who breaks the vicious cycles but Yahweh can only work through us. That's the deal.

---

drives us to strike out when threatened and, by extension, to seek revenge on those who harm us.

7. This assumes that we live in ordinary waking consciousness. Yahweh's ideal, a state of being in which we can truly love others as ourselves, is a metaphor for a higher level of consciousness, one that is in intimate communion with God and that transcends ego. The spiritual journey seeks that goal. Presumably, former muggers, rapists, and fraudsters would also reside in such a state.

19: 14
Don't Move the Corner Posts

You must not move your neighbor's boundary marker, set up by former generations, on the property that will be allotted to you in the land that the Lord your God is giving you to possess.

The economics of acquisitiveness runs roughshod over ancient entitlements. It does so in the name of progress and development, terms that mean, "There is money to be made." The making of money, however, is not to be slowed by pesky, vulnerable people with traditional rights that a bulldozer or court writ can run over.

This law in 19:14 is an absolute prohibition against moving boundary markers for personal gain; doing this damages someone else and so, harms the community. While the law is a defense of private property,[8] private property is part and parcel of the communal fabric. Since each piece of land is part of the larger "inheritance" of Israel, moving boundary markers cheats the whole community.

This simple law revisits the all-important basis of society: it precludes neighbor acting against neighbor. Taking it further, the law concerns neighbor versus neighbor plus the strong against the weak. The statute protects the small landholder when being preyed upon by more powerful economic agents. It prohibits land from being treated as a commodity, to be bought and sold, ultimately ending up in the hands of the rich and powerful.[9]

Again, we have to reflect on economic practices that line up big financial powers against the small and vulnerable. The Kingdom of God is not, and will not, be a place where powers overrun the entitlements of the vulnerable. Modern developers, be on notice!

---

8. "Personally held land" does not mean "owned." The land is owned by Yahweh. An individual takes care of it on behalf of the community.

9. This is not to say that "Small is beautiful" is necessarily good or that economy of scale is bad. Ten farmers with two acres each are likely to be less productive and efficient than ten farmers equitably farming twenty acres. The key word here is "equitable."

Deuteronomy and Post-Modern Christianity

19: 15–21
An Eye for an Eye vs. Turn the Other Cheek

> *A single witness shall not suffice to convict a person of any crime or wrongdoing in connection with any offense that may be committed. Only on the evidence of two or three witnesses shall a charge be sustained. 16 If a malicious witness comes forward to accuse someone of wrongdoing, 17 then both parties to the dispute shall appear before the Lord, before the priests and the judges who are in office in those days, 18 and the judges shall make a thorough inquiry. If the witness is a false witness, having testified falsely against another, 19 then you shall do to the false witness just as the false witness had meant to do to the other. So you shall purge the evil from your midst. 20 The rest shall hear and be afraid, and a crime such as this shall never again be committed among you. 21 Show no pity: life for life, eye for eye, tooth for tooth, hand for hand, foot for foot.*

The statute divides into two parts. The first part concerns a basic guideline that no one can be convicted of a crime on the testimony of one witness. This is a repeat of 17:6, emphasizing how important valid evidence is.

The second part of the text is of equally important concern: the unreliable witness who willfully misleads the court. Obviously, perjury will distort and discredit the entire judicial procedure. The offense of malicious witnesses is not simply that they lie, but rather that by lying, they willfully do damage to a neighbor. Again, this is all about protecting the neighbor. If the witness is found to be lying to do damage, he or she is punished. The law of retaliation is clear: The punishment fits the crime. Or, more precisely, the punishment fits the intended damage to the community. The cost of a crime (life for life, eye for eye, and the like) reflects an ancient system of penalties in which offenders were penalized.

Although we might think today that the eye-for-an-eye principle, the law of retaliation, is cruel, at the time of Deuteronomy, it was radically progressive. It was introduced to curb excessive cruelty among those bent on vengeance. Subsequently, an equally radical Jesus further modified the ethical traditions of Judaism, criticizing and overthrowing the principle of retaliation:

> *You have heard that it was said, "an eye for an eye and a tooth for a tooth." But I say to you, Do not resist an evildoer. But if anyone strikes you on the right cheek, turn the other also; and if anyone wants to sue you and take your coat, give your cloak as well; and*

if anyone forces you to go one mile, go also the second mile. Give to everyone who begs from you, and do not refuse anyone who wants to borrow from you. (Matt 5:38–42)

Deuteronomy intends to create an alternative community that practices measured justice that is not driven by bloodthirstiness. In turn, Jesus' teaching moves beyond the exact proportionality (an eye for an eye) of the Deuteronomic statute and summons a community that is an alternative to any violence, even the publicly sanctioned kind. This tension leaves open as future work the question of how to resist evil in a way that is genuinely transformative.

Chapter 11

How to Do a War

SINCE HUMANS FIRST MOVED out of Africa some fifty-thousand to one-hundred-thousand years ago, the Sinai peninsula has provided a highly fertile, easily accessed highway to the rest of the planet. It quickly became a main thoroughfare. As agriculture developed in this region, populations grew and competition for resources began in earnest. Mixing settled farmers with continuously encroaching nomads and migrants yielded a bubbling stew of conflict. The region became heavily populated with diverse groups and inevitably, tribal conflict became endemic. Deuteronomy 20, thus, provides rules for war.

The chapter makes clear, yet again, that Deuteronomy lives in the real world. In Deuteronomy 15, it moves in the world of *real debt*. In Deuteronomy 19, it moves in the world of *real murder*. Here, it acknowledges the world of *real war* and its accompanying hatred of the enemy and ensuing violence.

Deuteronomy knows that "War is hell" and is no less of a hell even if fought in the name of God. It would be gratifying if we could say in this chapter that war itself is in deep conflict with God. But, to the contrary, the writers know that we are of God. Since God can only act through us, God must necessarily be deeply enmeshed in barbarism. Although, with today's hindsight, we can see the underlying principles of nonviolence in Deuteronomy, the reality was that Israel did have to defend itself. The idea of Yahweh as a moral agent who stands against all violence had not yet developed; it still awaits development even today. At worst, violence in the name of God is no less common today. At best, we still engage in wars that we deem moral. An interesting dilemma, but nobody said that life is easy.

Deut 20: 1–9
Fear Not in War; God is Here

When you go out to war against your enemies, and see horses and chariots, an army larger than your own, you shall not be afraid of them; for the Lord your God is with you, who brought you up from the land of Egypt. ₂ Before you engage in battle, the priest shall come forward and speak to the troops, ₃ and shall say to them: "Hear, O Israel! Today you are drawing near to do battle against your enemies. Do not lose heart, or be afraid, or panic, or be in dread of them; ₄ for it is the Lord your God who goes with you, to fight for you against your enemies, to give you victory." ₅ Then the officials shall address the troops, saying, "Has anyone built a new house but not dedicated it? He should go back to his house, or he might die in the battle and another dedicate it. ₆ Has anyone planted a vineyard but not yet enjoyed its fruit? He should go back to his house, or he might die in the battle and another be first to enjoy its fruit. ₇ Has anyone become engaged to a woman but not yet married her? He should go back to his house, or he might die in the battle and another marry her." ₈ The officials shall continue to address the troops, saying, "Is anyone afraid or disheartened? He should go back to his house, or he might cause the heart of his comrades to melt like his own." ₉ When the officials have finished addressing the troops, then the commanders shall take charge of them.

The normal circumstance of war in Israel is that Israel may expect to be outnumbered and outgunned. The enemy will almost always have more troops and horses and chariots, and therefore, Israel will be afraid. It is not clear why this assumption is voiced. It might be rooted in some historical memory but remember, this is a story, not history. More likely, this assumption makes a good lead into verses 2 to 4. Here is a theological ploy. The "natural" response of fear in battle is countered by the reality of "the Lord your God," who can more than overcome any deficiency on Israel's part. They shall not be afraid because God is with them ("There are no atheists in foxholes"). The issue is not arms or troops; rather, it is a decision of fear or faith. Once again, the radical either/or of Deuteronomy appears concerning God's presence in the real affairs of the world.

After the priest's pep talk, the equivalent of today's military muster officer addresses the troops. This speech outlines four conditions for which one may be exempted from combat. The first three refer to unfinished business that might detract from full focus on the battle:

1. a new house still undedicated
2. a vineyard not yet enjoyed
3. a marriage not yet consummated.

These three provisions are highly practical because if such a male is away at war, another male will likely move in on his land and family and take over.

The fourth exemption in verse 8 is not truly about psychological fear but, again, about trusting in God or not.

Deut 20: 10–15
Israel Lays Siege, Yahweh Gives Victory

When you draw near to a town to fight against it, offer it terms of peace. $_{11}$ If it accepts your terms of peace and surrenders to you, then all the people in it shall serve you at forced labor. $_{12}$ If it does not submit to you peacefully, but makes war against you, then you shall besiege it; $_{13}$ and when the Lord your God gives it into your hand, you shall put all its males to the sword. $_{14}$ You may, however, take as your booty the women, the children, livestock, and everything else in the town, all its spoil. You may enjoy the spoil of your enemies, which the Lord your God has given you. $_{15}$ Thus you shall treat all the towns that are very far from you, which are not towns of the nations here.

Enough of the theological stuff. Let's get down to basics. This section of Deuteronomy probably derives from much older rules of war, common in that region at that time. The regulation is vicious and simple. In its approach to any enemy town, Israel must offer terms of surrender. The terms of peace are harsh: nothing less than complete surrender and forced labor. Presumably, an enemy would submit to such conditions only if it were very clear that Israel was going to win anyway.

If, on the other hand, the enemy resists this harsh offer of peace, Israel is then to unleash a siege. There is no doubt here that Israel will prevail over every enemy because Yahweh is the key factor in battle: Israel lays siege, Yahweh gives victory. The true interest here is not only the slaves that Israel brings home, but the additional booty it will get. Israel is to kill all opposing soldiers, but to take as war booty everything else, including women, children, and cattle; the former action removes the threat of retaliation at any time in the foreseeable future. The booty of livestock, as well as women and children slaves, is economically beneficial compared to slaughtering everyone.

This section of Deuteronomy is certainly barbaric by today's standards. Even though it makes us uncomfortable, we cannot deny that these basic rules of war were probably common to the ancient world. Are we truly any different now in modern warfare with its technologically enhanced brutality?

Deut 20: 16–18
Avoid the Abhorrent Ways of Other Peoples

> *But as for the towns of these peoples that the Lord your God is giving you as an inheritance, you must not let anything that breathes remain alive. $_{17}$ You shall annihilate them—the Hittites and the Amorites, the Canaanites and the Perizzites, the Hivites and the Jebusites—just as the Lord your God has commanded, $_{18}$ so that they may not teach you to do all the abhorrent things that they do for their gods, and you thus sin against the Lord your God.*

What went before was applicable only to distant towns and cities with which Israel is to have no continuing contact. There is a harsher requirement for towns close at hand, in the land of promise.

The Deuteronomists recognized that nearer towns presented a greater risk to Israel. Any remaining aspect of the culture or religion that was not annihilated could become seductive to the Israelites. It is possible to understand this provision as the rhetoric of faith gone hysterical and see it simply as ideology never intended to be embodied in actual war. We have to keep reminding ourselves that this is a story; the rhetoric of violence was intended to emphasize the single-mindedness required by Israel to maintain its distinctiveness. There is no evidence that any of the battles and slaughters cited ever happened, at least in a significant way.

Deuteronomy and Post-Modern Christianity

Deut 20: 19–20
Save Trees for Lumber and Food

> *If you besiege a town for a long time, making war against it in order to take it, you must not destroy its trees by wielding an ax against them. Although you may take food from them, you must not cut them down. Are trees in the field human beings that they should come under siege from you? 20 You may destroy only the trees that you know do not produce food; you may cut them down for use in building siegeworks against the town that makes war with you, until it falls.*

After the violence of verses 6 to 18, the final statute of verses 19 to 20 is surprising; it makes war environmentally friendly. Laying siege to a city was a widespread practice, and siege weapons require lumber. This need for lumber is one example of how war savages the environment and leaves land desolate and unproductive long after affairs of state have been resolved and forgotten.

In contrast to the previous realism regarding war, these final verses put an astonishing limitation on combat. The purpose is to protect the food chain and leave an after-battle food supply for enemies when Israel's troops have withdrawn. We might draw from this Israel's recognition that the created world has its own rights and privileges; important limitations are imposed on human intervention.

Characteristic of Deuteronomy, this chapter on war combines passionate Yahwistic faith with harsh social policy. No doubt the pressure and anxiety of real circumstances initially produced this severity. In any case, Yahweh is fully drawn into this harshness and is viewed as making it legitimate.

Deuteronomy does not deny a thirst for war but does smoothly change it into a summons to faith. Although Israel may not have been the first to claim that God was on its side in war, this ancient writing certainly provides the same self-serving, self-deceiving legitimization that nations use today. For example, the United States deeply links its military power to "God" so that seemingly endless waves of invasion and violence are justified as God's will against evil. Ironically, the Christian scriptures (the New Testament) provide a testimony of suffering love which keeps speaking against violence. Maybe it is time for the connection of *faith and fight* to change to having enough faith *not* to fight, but instead, to risk other actions in obedience, thereby, creating a new future.

Chapter 12

How to Be Neighborly

THE NEXT GROUP OF laws in Deuteronomy is random and seems to have no structure. The intention is to bring every phase of Israel's life under Yahweh and the covenant.

Deut 21: 1–9
Slay a Heifer to Absolve Bloodguilt

> *If, in the land that the Lord your God is giving you to possess, a body is found lying in open country, and it is not known who struck the person down, ₂ then your elders and your judges shall come out to measure the distances to the towns that are near the body. ₃ The elders of the town nearest the body shall take a heifer that has never been worked, one that has not pulled in the yoke; ₄ the elders of that town shall bring the heifer down to a wadi with running water, which is neither plowed nor sown, and shall break the heifer's neck there in the wadi. ₅ Then the priests, the sons of Levi, shall come forward, for the Lord your God has chosen them to minister to him and to pronounce blessings in the name of the Lord, and by their decision all cases of dispute and assault shall be settled. ₆ All the elders of that town nearest the body shall wash their hands over the heifer whose neck was broken in the wadi, ₇ and they shall declare: "Our hands did not shed this blood, nor were we witnesses to it. ₈ Absolve, O Lord, your people Israel, whom you redeemed; do not let the guilt of innocent blood remain in the midst of your people Israel." Then they will be absolved of bloodguilt.*

The first statute fits well under the law "Do not kill." It is concerned with bloodguilt and the shedding of innocent blood but here the problem is different from the earlier laws because there is no one who can identify the killer. The closest town is given jurisdiction and has to take responsibility to declare that it is innocent. The elders of the town do this through two speeches, one of declaration and one of petition. This is likely a very old, traditional practice, surely older than Yahwehism because there is no reference to Yahweh. The elders assert that neither they nor anyone from the village have shed the blood or witnessed its shedding. This distances the elders and their village from the bloodguilt. This well-ordered protocol gives the community security and well-being in the face of the unknown.

Deut 21: 10–14
A Man May Take a Captive Woman as Bride

> *When you go out to war against your enemies, and the Lord your God hands them over to you and you take them captive, 11 suppose you see among the captives a beautiful woman whom you desire and want to marry, 12 and so you bring her home to your house: she shall shave her head, pare her nails, 13 discard her captive's garb, and shall remain in your house a full month, mourning for her father and mother; after that you may go in to her and be her husband, and she shall be your wife. 14 But if you are not satisfied with her, you shall let her go free and not sell her for money. You must not treat her as a slave, since you have dishonored her.*

There was no Geneva Convention in those days. Today, we wouldn't do this (unless, of course, we were the victorious army). Warriors are free to "want" and to "take" foreign women in war. The woman has no voice in the matter, either to resist or comply. The man, who has all of the rights, acts upon her. If he desires, he takes; if he no longer desires, he sends out. Male power affirms that he is free to marry and divorce the woman whom he has forcibly seized. The law clearly assumes a male-dominated situation. While it defines the woman's legal status, as wife, and provides her protection in that status (she may not be sold), it does so by limiting the *man's* actions.

Evidently, Deuteronomy has not yet applied the equality of the covenant to women as it has done in other matters such as the economy.

Deut 21: 15–17
The Firstborn Son Retains Rights of Inheritance

If a man has two wives, one of them loved and the other disliked, and if both the loved and the disliked have borne him sons, the firstborn being the son of the one who is disliked, 16 then on the day when he wills his possessions to his sons, he is not permitted to treat the son of the loved as the firstborn in preference to the son of the disliked, who is the firstborn. 17 He must acknowledge as firstborn the son of the one who is disliked, giving him a double portion of all that he has; since he is the first issue of his virility, the right of the firstborn is his.

This statute concerns the right of inheritance. It is designed to protect the privilege of the firstborn son in the inheritance of family property. In that ancient world and well into the modern world, this custom is intended to protect family property, to prevent endless quarrels about inheritance of land, and to preclude the fragmentation of such property with a multiplicity of heirs.

The landowner cannot give privileges to the younger son and throw over social convention. So says Moses, because such an act would not be right. It would violate just entitlement. This teaching supports traditionalism against any favoritism, even by the male head of the family. This is an important distinction. In spite of patriarchal authority, the father is regulated in the interest of social stability.

Deut 21: 18–21
Stone to Death Any Rebellious Son

If someone has a stubborn and rebellious son who will not obey his father and mother, who does not heed them when they discipline him, 19 then his father and his mother shall take hold of him and bring him out to the elders of his town at the gate of that place. 20 They shall say to the elders of his town, "This son of ours is stubborn and rebellious. He will not obey us. He is a glutton and a drunkard." 21 Then all the men of the town shall stone him to death. So you shall purge the evil from your midst; and all Israel will hear, and be afraid.

Probably most of us who are parents have, at some moment of terrible frustration, fleetingly wished that this law was still around. The statute affirms traditional parental authority over children in the interest of maintaining social order. With the son a disturbance, such misconduct brings shame on the family and eventual economic jeopardy to the community. Such a family crisis, therefore, is a public concern. Public execution would certainly set an example to others who might want unrestrained freedom. Again, this is probably a very early law.

Deut 21: 22–23
Execute and Bury a Criminal on the Same Day

When someone is convicted of a crime punishable by death and is executed, and you hang him on a tree, ₂₃ his corpse must not remain all night upon the tree; you shall bury him that same day, for anyone hung on a tree is under God's curse. You must not defile the land that the Lord your God is giving you for possession.

This law is about the land, not the body. It's possible that the powers of death that swirl around the body are thought to pose a special threat at night, and therefore, burial is required. Or it might be that sundown sets a limit on the time of exposure, because a decomposed body intrinsically poses a threat. In any case, a dead body of one executed for a crime is an affront to God and a threat to the community. There are, no doubt, all sorts of possible meanings to the words "death, night, and curse" in this text but they have been lost.

Deut 22: 1–4
Recover Your Neighbor's Lost Livestock and Goods

You shall not watch your neighbor's ox or sheep straying away and ignore them; you shall take them back to their owner. ₂ If the owner does not reside near you or you do not know who the owner is, you shall bring it to your own house, and it shall remain with you until the owner claims it; then you shall return it. ₃ You shall do the same with a neighbor's donkey; you shall do the same with a neighbor's garment; and you shall do the same with anything else that your neighbor loses and you find. You may not withhold your help. ₄ You shall not see your neighbor's donkey or ox fallen on the road and ignore it; you shall help to lift it up.

Deuteronomy and Post-Modern Christianity

Deuteronomy was written for small farming communities, small landholders who depend on each other daily for cooperation, assistance, and vigilance. These four statutes concern the responsibility of the neighbor to return what is lost when it is found; neighbors are bound together in mutual care and protection. The most remarkable aspect of this group of rules is the one that says: "You may not withhold your help." You may not hide yourself. You may not withdraw from neighborliness. Perhaps in a more contemporary context, you may not live behind high walls in a gated community, as though you are not obligated to be a neighbor.

Once again, we are reminded that this is God's dream for us. This is the ideal society, what it means to love others as you love yourself. It is a far reach but we know it is what we *should* be striving for. The claims of God extend to the most mundane realities of daily life.

Deut 22: 5–12
Keep Things in Their Proper Place for Right Living

A woman shall not wear a man's apparel, nor shall a man put on a woman's garment; for whoever does such things is abhorrent to the Lord your God. 6 If you come on a bird's nest, in any tree or on the ground, with fledglings or eggs, with the mother sitting on the fledglings or on the eggs, you shall not take the mother with the young. 7 Let the mother go, taking only the young for yourself, in order that it may go well with you and you may live long. 8 When you build a new house, you shall make a parapet for your roof; otherwise you might have bloodguilt on your house, if anyone should fall from it. 9 You shall not sow your vineyard with a second kind of seed, or the whole yield will have to be forfeited, both the crop that you have sown and the yield of the vineyard itself. 10 You shall not plow with an ox and a donkey yoked together. 11 You shall not wear clothes made of wool and linen woven together. 12 You shall make tassels on the four corners of the cloak with which you cover yourself.

This is an intriguing group of rules, similar to the "and other duties as assigned" section of a job description. We have a bit of ecology, an early attempt at a building code, and something about decorating your cloak. There is a general theme as well, about mixing things that should be kept apart. We truly don't know the stories behind any of these prohibitions. Obviously, some very old traditions are at play here. It would seem that the Deuteronomists worried that any deviation from old traditions, regardless if they made sense or not, could open the flood gates to all sorts of deviance from "right living."

A reader at the beginning of the twenty-first century might especially notice the insistence on investment in the community. The ideology of privatization and individual rights leads to self-indulgence, the unwillingness to focus on the neighbor, and the reluctance to pay tax money for the common good. Such rampant individualism indicates a yearning to do away with neighborliness and, as we see today especially in North America, the erosion of neighborliness leads to fragmentation of community, fear and further isolation. A vicious cycle. In contrast, the ancient wisdom of Deuteronomy insists that the future depends upon sustained, intentional commitment to the public good.

Deut 22: 13–30
In Sexual Relations, Male Power and Privilege Reign

Suppose a man marries a woman, but after going in to her, he dislikes her $_{14}$ and makes up charges against her, slandering her by saying, "I married this woman; but when I lay with her, I did not find evidence of her virginity." $_{15}$ The father of the young woman and her mother shall then submit the evidence of the young woman's virginity to the elders of the city at the gate. $_{16}$ The father of the young woman shall say to the elders: "I gave my daughter in marriage to this man but he dislikes her; $_{17}$ now he has made up charges against her, saying, 'I did not find evidence of your daughter's virginity.' But here is the evidence of my daughter's virginity."

Then they shall spread out the cloth before the elders of the town. $_{18}$ The elders of that town shall take the man and punish him; $_{19}$ they shall fine him one hundred shekels of silver (which they shall give to the young woman's father) because he has slandered a virgin of Israel. She shall remain his wife; he shall not be permitted to divorce her as long as he lives. $_{20}$ If, however, this charge is true, that evidence of the young woman's virginity was not found, $_{21}$ then they shall bring the young woman out to the entrance of her father's house and the men of her town shall stone her to death, because she committed a disgraceful act in Israel by prostituting herself in her father's house. So you shall purge the evil from your midst. $_{22}$ If a man is caught lying with the wife of another man, both of them shall die, the man who lay with the woman as well as the woman. So you shall purge

> the evil from Israel. ₂₃ If there is a young woman, a virgin already engaged to be married, and a man meets her in the town and lies with her, ₂₄ you shall bring both of them to the gate of that town and stone them to death, the young woman because she did not cry for help in the town and the man because he violated his neighbor's wife. So you shall purge the evil from your midst. ₂₅ But if the man meets the engaged woman in the open country, and the man seizes her and lies with her, then only the man who lay with her shall die. ₂₆ You shall do nothing to the young woman; the young woman has not committed an offense punishable by death, because this case is like that of someone who attacks and murders a neighbor. ₂₇ Since he found her in the open country, the engaged woman may have cried for help, but there was no one to rescue her. ₂₈ If a man meets a virgin who is not engaged, and seizes her and lies with her, and they are caught in the act, ₂₉ the man who lay with her shall give fifty shekels of silver to the young woman's father, and she shall become his wife. Because he violated her he shall not be permitted to divorce her as long as he lives. ₃₀ A man shall not marry his father's wife, thereby violating his father's rights.

These six statutes seek to regulate sexual relationships between a man and a woman. But we notice right off that that there is no mention of Yahweh throughout. Undoubtedly, these rules come from a much more ancient tradition. Nevertheless, in spite of the brilliance and forward thinking that the Deuteronomists have exhibited in other matters, it is clear here once again that the concept of equality between the sexes is still a long way off. The regulations governing sexual relationships are intensely patriarchal, written from a male perspective to protect male entitlements and privileges. Indeed, even in the case of the violation of a woman, it is forbidden not because of her self-worth but because she related to another man; therefore, the affront is to the man. The only bright spot here seems to be the recurring emphasis on the rule of law regarding disputes. Nonetheless, the resolution of the dispute regarding the virginity of the wife is a man-to-man deal, with the woman simply a passive party, like damaged goods.

And it gets worse. Verses 20 to 21 are willing to entertain the alternative that the husband's charge is true and the woman is not a virgin. In that case, severe reaction against the woman is authorized. She has done "a disgraceful thing in Israel" by violating her virginity, bringing shame to her family, humiliation to her husband, and jeopardy to her community. Every cohesive village society knows about the scandal of such an act and the deep shame that comes upon the entire household for a daughter's failure to be a "good girl." The text conjures a scene of unrestrained male violence against a woman who has dared to disrupt a social order that guarantees a network of male power.

Without question, by today's western standards, Deuteronomy has erred in this matter. Right up to the present time, Jewish and Christian communities have perpetuated this patriarchal power, claiming to have divine authority enshrined in the Bible. Ironically, it is good that for the most part, our secular society has ignored religion in this respect and given rise to the feminist movement. In this area, the faith communities have failed miserably and are still scrambling to catch up with society.

Religion might still be able to make contributions in a dehumanized society, but not through direct appeal to texts such as these. As emphasized much earlier, Deuteronomy was never intended to be taken at face value. Anyone serious about spiritual development knows that all the scriptures are best understood through a continuing interpretive practice that always moves between traditional inheritances and faithful innovation of a covenantal kind. That's what we call discernment.

Chapter 13

Who's In and Who's Out

DEUTERONOMY SETS UP A community devoted unreservedly to Yahweh. Members are to be a holy people of trust and obedience. The writers have gone to great lengths to describe such a generous community in detail. All are to share and hold equal value regardless of their social status or wealth. Even the lowest—the widow, the orphan, the slave—are to be treated fairly, with proper care also given to the alien or stranger.

Given that aim, who is and is not in the community is important. If one is said to be an insider to the covenant community, then others must be outsiders, excluded to maintain the integrity of the community. That creates a dilemma: You're told to love your neighbor as yourself, but have to decide who exactly is and is not your neighbor. There is no doubt, therefore, that in post-exile Judaism, the question of exclusiveness was acute. This had to be a very special club; not just anyone could join. To protect the community in its purity, the rules said that foreigners were disqualified simply because they were foreigners.

Deut 23: 1–8
Don't Exclude the Egyptians

No one whose testicles are crushed or whose penis is cut off shall be admitted to the assembly of the Lord. ₂ Those born of an illicit union shall not be admitted to the assembly of the Lord. Even to the tenth generation, none of their descendants shall be admitted to the assembly of the Lord. ₃ No Ammonite or Moabite shall be admitted to the assembly of the Lord. Even to the tenth generation, none of their descendants shall be admitted to the assembly of the Lord, ₄ because they did not meet you with food and water on your journey

Who's In and Who's Out

> out of Egypt, and because they hired against you Balaam son of Beor, from Pethor of Mesopotamia, to curse you. ₅ (Yet the Lord your God refused to heed Balaam; the Lord your God turned the curse into a blessing for you, because the Lord your God loved you.) ₆ You shall never promote their welfare or their prosperity as long as you live. ₇ You shall not abhor any of the Edomites, for they are your kin. You shall not abhor any of the Egyptians, because you were an alien residing in their land. ₈ The children of the third generation that are born to them may be admitted to the assembly of the Lord.

This section presents guidelines for exclusion. The first two guidelines concern Israelites whom the community might normally admit but who are rejected. Reference to male genitalia indicates how closely membership is related to the ability to procreate, a pervasive concern of the ancestral narratives in Genesis. The second rule of disqualification of an Israelite concerns someone born out of wedlock. This rule of exclusion reinforces the rules on illicit sexuality in chapter 22.

The next group of exclusions is ethnic and concerns, in turn, the Ammonites, Moabites, Edomites, and Egyptians. While these exclusionary rules are stated absolutely, we have to assume that these four groups just happened to be on the bad-people list when this was written. A different century, presumably, would have given us a different list.

Israel's cousins Ammon and Moab (see Gen 19:30–38) are excluded from the assembly forever. Why? Apparently, they refused others food and water, thereby violating the rules of hospitality. Some historical memory is likely at work here, rendering an affront so awful that forgiveness would never be possible.

The Edomites get off more lightly but it is not clear why. Obviously, whatever they did wrong to Israel was not in the same category as actions by the Ammonites and Moabites. This still remains short of a welcome but the community, at least, will allow in the third generation. Remember: All of these groups had been co-habiting the same region for centuries. This is truly nothing more than tribal politics.

Finally, comes the astonishing affirmation of the fourth people mentioned, the Egyptians. After the abusiveness of the pharaoh, one might have expected hostility toward Egypt. But apparently, Deuteronomy remembers Egypt here simply as the metaphorical host country of the ancestors and not as an abuser.

Deuteronomy and Post-Modern Christianity

While exclusion has been a primary posture in shaping Judaism, it has not been without important challenges. In the book of Ruth, the Moabite Ruth becomes an Israelite and eventually, a mother to the later king David (see Ruth 4:13–22 and Matt 1:5). More important, Isa 56:3–8 affirms that all eunuchs and foreigners are welcomed into the community of covenant if they subscribe to covenant and practice sabbath.

The same critical question that occupied emerging Judaism inevitably surfaced in early Christianity (see Acts 15). This old tension of exclusion and inclusion continues in our modern age.

Chapter 14

The Summation

Deut 26: 1–19
Bringing it all Together

When you have come into the land that the Lord your God is giving you as an inheritance to possess, and you possess it, and settle in it, ₂ you shall take some of the first of all the fruit of the ground, which you harvest from the land that the Lord your God is giving you, and you shall put it in a basket and go to the place that the Lord your God will choose as a dwelling for his name. ₃ You shall go to the priest who is in office at that time, and say to him, "Today I declare to the Lord your God that I have come into the land that the Lord swore to our ancestors to give us." ₄ When the priest takes the basket from your hand and sets it down before the altar of the Lord your God, ₅ you shall make this response before the Lord your God: "A wandering Aramean was my ancestor; he went down into Egypt and lived there as an alien, few in number, and there he became a great nation, mighty and populous. ₆ When the Egyptians treated us harshly and afflicted us, by imposing hard labor on us, ₇ we cried to the Lord, the God of our ancestors; the Lord heard our voice and saw our affliction, our toil, and our oppression. ₈ The Lord brought us out of Egypt with a mighty hand and an outstretched arm, with a terrifying display of power, and with signs and wonders; ₉ and he brought us into this place and gave us this land, a land flowing with milk and honey. ₁₀ So now I bring the first of the fruit of the ground that you, O Lord, have given me." You shall set it down before the Lord your God and bow down before the Lord your God. ₁₁ Then you, together with the Levites and the aliens who reside among you, shall celebrate with all the bounty that the Lord your God has given to you and to

Deuteronomy and Post-Modern Christianity

> your house. 12 When you have finished paying all the tithe of your produce in the third year (which is the year of the tithe), giving it to the Levites, the aliens, the orphans, and the widows, so that they may eat their fill within your towns, 13 then you shall say before the Lord your God: "I have removed the sacred portion from the house, and I have given it to the Levites, the resident aliens, the orphans, and the widows, in accordance with your entire commandment that you commanded me; I have neither transgressed nor forgotten any of your commandments: 14 I have not eaten of it while in mourning; I have not removed any of it while I was unclean; and I have not offered any of it to the dead. I have obeyed the Lord my God, doing just as you commanded me. 15 Look down from your holy habitation, from heaven, and bless your people Israel and the ground that you have given us, as you swore to our ancestors—a land flowing with milk and honey." 16 This very day the Lord your God is commanding you to observe these statutes and ordinances; so observe them diligently with all your heart and with all your soul. 17 Today you have obtained the Lord's agreement: to be your God; and for you to walk in his ways, to keep his statutes, his commandments, and his ordinances, and to obey him. 18 Today the Lord has obtained your agreement: to be his treasured people, as he promised you, and to keep his commandments; 19 for him to set you high above all nations that he has made, in praise and in fame and in honor; and for you to be a people holy to the Lord your God, as he promised.

This chapter brings us to the end of the middle speech of Moses. In summing up, Deuteronomy tells us once again to love God absolutely and to love our neighbor absolutely. We can only sit in awe at this point. Think back for a few moments and consider the span of this speech: the oneness of God, the Ten Commandments, the institution of the Sabbath, the sense that all humans are equal and precious, the demand that Yahweh be totally kept up front in every aspect of life, the equitable distribution of food, the appropriate conduct of war, the ending of cycles of violence, the implementation of social justice, the absolute limits put on the powerful in their dealings with the poor, it goes on and on. What amazing concepts the writers had to struggle with.

And interestingly, even though it was compiled so long ago, Deuteronomy will not leave us alone today: it wrestles throughout with good and evil. Of course, most sacred writings address this basic issue but Deuteronomy does so in a very down to earth manner that remains totally relevant

The Summation

to us today. Thus, Deuteronomy calls out for reflection, indeed, serious reflection for the rest of our lives.

Let's pause a moment therefore and briefly consider the issue of good and evil and God. To do so from a post-modern theological perspective we have to start with something even more basic, life's big questions: Who are we? Why do we exist? Where did all this come from?

Our physical being evolved from primordial protoplasm over millions of years, along with all other living organisms. At one end of the spectrum, that of the vast universe itself, today's cosmology says that perhaps our universe is infinite or, alternatively, there might be many universes. Maybe the Big Bang is cyclical, occurring over and over again. Time and space could be one and the same. In all likelihood, other intelligent life forms are "out there." Meanwhile, at the other end, the submicroscopic end of the spectrum, string theory indicates that there might be twelve dimensions, not just four. Particles of matter are simultaneously energy waves. There is nothing definitive about photons, just probabilities about how they behave. Time and space may not be continuous but, rather, tiny chunky bits. Although these suppositions are intriguing, they still do not answer life's big questions nor is there anything about good and evil or even God. Perhaps instead we have to look elsewhere, outside of time/space.

Certainly, we evolved physically along with all other life forms. Yet, there remains a vast gulf between us and other animals. Only a few thousand years ago,[1] *homo sapiens* developed self-consciousness, cultural memory, and empathy for others; these aspects of life far outstripped physical evolution. Through this self-awareness, we began to "know" that we were not alone. We became aware of Spirit. From that sprang a sense of love, greater truth, and goodness.[2] Ultimately, we can describe these senses only as mystery. Although we can measure the distance to stars and attempt to describe the smallest particles that make up our universe, we cannot begin to describe or measure truth, goodness, and love. We experience them. We know and act on them constantly even though they are far beyond the physical universe and the grasp of our rational minds. They become inseparable from other experiences that we call God, such as eternal, unchanging wisdom. The *experience* of God has not changed over the millennia, only

---

1. Estimates range anywhere between 3000 and 5000 BCE.
2. Knowing good implies we know evil as well. Good remains in the realm of mystery but evil (the absence of good) might be attributed in time/space to aberrant DNA or wrong brain wiring. See Chapter 6, commentary on Deuteronomy 8.

our intellectual understanding of God. We have found that life's mystery, the mystery of God, can only be tamed or made accessible through mythology. Fortunately, we have inherited the Hebrew mythology, more commonly known as the Hebrew scriptures or the Old Testament of the Bible, which addresses the "absolutes" of life so beautifully and directly.[3] We ignore it at our peril because Hebrew mythology is truly the mythology of western Europe and North America. For that reason we return to Deuteronomy.

Deuteronomy is nothing less than revolutionary, not only for its own time but also for the enduring effect it has had on western culture. It is a vision of the ideal, one that we can imagine. Judaism, Islam, and Christianity have all glimpsed this ideal and share it as the ultimate goal: Paradise, the Land of Milk and Honey, the Kingdom of God. That goal is to be obtained here and now—it has nothing to do with the afterlife.

Nevertheless, in spite of Deuteronomy's idealism, it is immensely practical. It deals with day-to-day issues that we continuously face as we try to live in community. Over and over, the Deuteronomists point out that there is nothing idealistic about ownership, power over others, anger, revenge, shame, and greed. These traits were the grist in the mill of our forbearers and remain so even today, three thousand years later. Ownership, power, anger, greed are comfortable places to be, places of great familiarity. Attempting to overcome them is an ongoing struggle.

But it is not hopeless. Underneath Deuteronomy's theology is the recognition of a universal, foundational "good," a universal Truth, an Absolute, a pure Love that underpins our whole existence. Such is God's dream for us.

So simple and yet so profound. Other than some references to ritualistic practice, there are no required beliefs, no miracles. It is just the straight goods, the essence of what we can become. This is where post-modern Christianity heads, back to the real Jesus of Nazareth, the rabbi, the teacher, the healer, the reformer. Jesus, in turn, referred back to Moses and spoke not of the letter of the law—which is so much easier to live—but of the spirit of the law—which is so much more difficult to live. Jesus of Nazareth was not the literal "Son of God," he was not "sent" by God to be a sacrifice for our sins. Rather, Jesus was a mystic. He lived a real life but he lived that life in the full consciousness of God. His life personified that which the

---

3. Although we study and expound upon Greek mythology, it is the down-to-earth Hebrew mythology that addresses our real-life experiences. And the change in our intellectual understanding? Simply the recognition that although mythology contains truth, it is not factual.

The Summation

Deuteronomists taught through the tradition of Moses. And he wanted all people to grow into that ideal. Yes, the teachings of Jesus were constrained by the culture of his time and place but he would never say that we are sinners in the sense that we are judged by a deity in the sky. We are human, made in God's image, struggling with good and bad, seeking the God we know as love. Post-modern Christianity is a new, very old idea and we might even say that Jesus was the first post-modern Christian. We can do away with dogma, having to believe, needing forgiveness from "out there." Jesus was not about that. We need forgiveness from ourselves.

Jesus said it well: Love God and love your neighbor. Post-modern Christianity says exactly the same thing: Open your hearts and minds to God. The Kingdom of God, the enlightenment, the peace that passes all understanding will be ours. This is the challenge of Christianity and all other religions. We do not need to be told how to live. We need simply to strengthen our spiritual connection with the love we call God. The rest will fall out by itself, as a naturally occurring way of living.

Annotated Bibliography

THE FOLLOWING BOOKS AND authors are recommended for those who wish to further pursue their understanding of post-modern Christianity. There is no claim made here that this is a comprehensive reading list or the best one in the world. It does comprise, though, a good two years of reading and study. You may never be the same again!

Akenson, Donald Harman, *Saint Saul*. Toronto, Ont.: Oxford University Press, 2002.

> Akenson is an historian who applies his discipline to the origin and development of the Bible. This book is a spin-off from *Surpassing Wonder*, but focused on Paul. It makes an excellent study of this apostle. If you read this first, you will immediately get *Surpassing Wonder* when you finish it.

Akenson, Donald Harman, *Surpassing Wonder: The Invention of the Bible*. Montreal, Que.: McGill-Queens, 1995.

> This is much more scholarly than the work of Borg or Spong but is very readable. The author's passion for the Bible shows through, along with his sense of humor. This is everything you will ever need to know about the history of the Bible. A great book.

Borg, Marcus J. *Meeting Jesus Again for the First Time*. New York, NY: HarperCollins, 1995.

Borg, Marcus J. *The Heart of Christianity*. New York, NY: HarperCollins, 2004.

> A comprehensive but highly readable discussion of what is essentially post-modern Christianity, although the book does not use this term. Both of these books cover pretty much the same materials as the Spong books. Some people prefer Spong, others Borg.

Brueggemann, Walter. *Deuteronomy*. Nashville, Tenn.: Abingdon, 2001.

> His writing is very scholarly but most worthwhile, for the brave. He makes the Old Testament come alive and offers many great profound insights into these remarkable writings.

Annotated Bibliography

Brueggemann, Walter. *Prophetic Imagination*. Philadelphia, Pa.: Fortress, 1978.

> By deeply examining the prophets, Brueggemann develops the idea that Moses and Jesus lived in an altered state of God-consciousness. This can change your whole thinking about God.

Brueggemann, Walter. *Theology of the Old Testament*. Minneapolis, Minn.: Fortress, 1997.

> Reading this will help you begin to think that modern Christianity truly misses the boat by not taking the Old Testament a lot more seriously. There is nothing in the New Testament that is not in the Old Testament.

Capon, Robert Farrer. *The Third Peacock: The Problem of God and Evil*. Toronto, Ont.: HarperCollins, 1986.

> This whimsical, lyrical book explores the concept of God as lover rather than favor-granter. This is one of the earlier writings of Capon, a serious theologian.

Crossan, John Dominic, and Reed, Jonathon L. *Excavating Jesus: Beneath the Stones, Behind the Texts*. New York, NY: HarperCollins, 2001.

> This in-depth look at the world of Jesus by two scholars provides insight into the origin of related events. Be warned: This is not light reading. However, it is essential to understanding where Christianity comes from and why post-modern Christians look so intensely at this particular period.

Dowd, Michael. *Thank God for Evolution: How the Marriage of Science and Religion Will Transform Your Life and Our World*. New York, NY: Viking Penguin Group, 2009.

> This book offers a rare mix of serious science and serious theology. It explores in detail how our brain stem makes it difficult for us to attain the alternative state of consciousness called the Kingdom of Heaven or "the land of milk and honey."

Finkelstein, Israel and Silberman, Neil Asher. *The Bible unearthed: archaeology's new vision of ancient Israel and the origin of its sacred texts*. New York, NY: Simon and Schuster, 2002.

> A Jewish theologian and archeologist combine their expertise to investigate what current archaeology says about ancient Israel and the origin of its sacred texts. This is a fascinating book and a delightful read.

Annotated Bibliography

Fishbane, Michael. *Sacred Attunement: A Jewish Theology.* Chicago, Ill.: The University of Chicago Press, 2008.

This presents a serious look at current Jewish theology or post-modern Judaism. Although not an easy read, it is remarkably beautiful, almost poetic, and certainly mystical. Partway through or at the end of this book, the following question will undoubtedly pop into your mind: How does post-modern Judaism differ from post-modern Christianity? That's a good question.

McFague, Sally. *Life Abundant: Rethinking Theology and Economy for a Planet in Peril.* Minneapolis, NM: Augsburg Fortress, 2001.

Both a theologian and ecologist, the author offers a concise post-modern theology and how closely it relates to human impact on the ecology of our planet.

Pagels, Elaine. *The Gnostic Gospels.* New York, NY: Random House, 1979.

The author outlines how the theology of the Gnostics was suppressed by the Roman church.

Spong, John Shelby. *Born of a Woman.* New York, NY: HarperCollins, 1994.

Quite a comprehensive look at the birth narratives, how and why they developed. Bishop Spong is not an academic per se, but in many ways, he was a pioneer in popularizing and making available to the average person some of the current thinking of the serious Judeo-Christian theologians. His writing is an excellent source for the novice seeker.

Spong, John Shelby. *Liberating the Gospels: Reading the Bible with Jewish Eyes.* New York, NY: HarperCollins, 1997.

This explores a hypothesis that the gospels were written to fit with the Jewish liturgical calendar. It is a heavy read but worth it.

Spong, John Shelby. *Rescuing the Bible from Fundamentalism.* New York, NY: HarperCollins, 1992.

This is an excellent introduction to current thinking about the origins of the Bible and the issues that many Christians have with modern Christianity. This will whet your appetite.

Spong, John Shelby. *Resurrection: Myth or Reality.* New York, NY: HarperCollins, 1995.

It offers a post-modern look at the resurrection.

www.ingramcontent.com/pod-product-compliance
Lightning Source LLC
Chambersburg PA
CBHW070925160426
43193CB00011B/1580